DISCOVERING THE YORKSHIRE DALES

Discovering the Yorkshire Dales

*Its Hidden Places, Curiosities and Strange Events
with John Ward*

First published in 1996 by

Smith Settle Ltd
Ilkley Road
Otley
West Yorkshire
LS21 3JP

© John Ward 1996

ISBN 1 85825 051 X

British Library Cataloguing-in-Publication Data:
A catalogue record is available for this book
from the British Library.

Opening page: Pepper Pot, Swinithwaite
Title page: Kettlewell

Set in Souvenir

Designed, printed and bound by
SMITH SETTLE
Ilkley Road, Otley, West Yorkshire LS21 3JP

Contents

Settle Area

The Far North-West

Richmond and Swaledale

Lower Wensleydale

Upper Wensleydale

Introduction

I left the Dales when I was eighteen and returned over forty years later.

It was a return which I had long set my heart on, which I increasingly yearned for as the years went by and, when it came, was a return to a land of sheer delight.

It had been a world apart, isolated from the changes in much of England, and to some degree that was still true, but the Dales is no longer an island. Visitors invade it in their thousands and very welcome they are too, so long as their sheer numbers do not destroy what they come to discover. They come to walk on its lonely stretches of heather moorland, by its massive limestone escarpments or in the valleys of the dales, not one of which is like another.

It is a land of infinite variety.

They also come to see its man-made treasures, and they too are so varied and plentiful that no man can know them all. In assembling this collection I have avoided the great abbeys of Fountains, Jervaulx and the like; they are indeed not only treasures of the Dales but treasures of the world. If you have time to visit but one of these places, there can only be one choice. It has to be Fountains Abbey, but see it when the crowds are not there and you can feel its peace. I have also avoided the great castles of Richmond, Middleham, Bolton and Skipton, and the splendid local museums such as Hawes and Pateley Bridge. All of these are essential ingredients of an extended stay in the Dales.

Essential, too, are some of the Dales churches. Sadly, vandalism has led to the closure of many of them for much of the week, but take pot luck and you will not be disappointed. A few of them, as well as a number of vernacular houses, have been included in my collection. I love them, could not possibly leave them out and could easily have included more.

The collection, which is inevitably a personal one, also includes people, some of the natural riches of the Dales, and some of its rarities and eccentricities.

The area covered is also, to a degree, a personal choice. Clearly it has to include the Yorkshire Dales National Park and the recently, and belatedly, designated Area of Outstanding Natural Beauty, which ought to be in the National Park, but I have ventured somewhat further than that, particularly to the east, where my boundary is roughly along the line from Richmond to Ripon to Knaresborough. Most people would consider those towns to be within the Dales. On the other hand, Harrogate, grand, beautiful and full of interest as it is, is not a Dales town and, with apologies to its citizens, I have left it out. In any event it deserves a book of treasures and curiosities all to itself.

As for my collection, I have tried to indicate how you might get to them and, for those who use such things, I have given map references. All 112 are accessible by car or by a short easy walk from a car. They have been arranged in eleven sections, each of which would make a stimulating day-long excursion into the Dales. A simple schematic map at the beginning of each section gives the locations of the sites in relation to one another, and an overall map of the Dales (overleaf) means you can easily see if the place you are visiting holds something of interest. (North is at the top of the page on all the maps.) The last section deals with those 'universal' treasures which can be found all over the Dales. The reference numbers used in all the maps and index refer to the page on which the particular item appears.

My thanks are due to Richmond's Georgian Theatre for permission to reproduce the photograph of the theatre's interior on page 63, and to the Ripon Prison and Police Museum for the photo of one of their reconstructed cells on page 98.

So, *bon voyage*, immerse yourself in the landscape and let it fill your senses, marvel at some of man's achievements and have fun at some of his foibles.

In your travels round the Dales you will find much more to wonder at and amuse. If you read something of its life and history you will enjoy it all the more. Wherever I am, I like to think of it as it might have looked when the great abbeys owned most of the land and their granges were scattered everywhere. I like to think, too, of it more recently when smoke from lime-burning rose in the air from a thousand kilns, when textile mills lined the valleys, when pack-horse trains carrying coal, lead, salt and all kinds of goods criss-crossed the land and when men, women and children — industrial workers all — walked miles to and from their work in lead and coal mines. Keep these things in mind and you begin to appreciate how the Dales became like they are today.

May this book serve as a introduction and may you, before long, decide as I did long ago that the Dales are treasures beyond price.

Look after them.

John Ward
Ilkley, 1996

Overall Map of the Yorkshire Dales

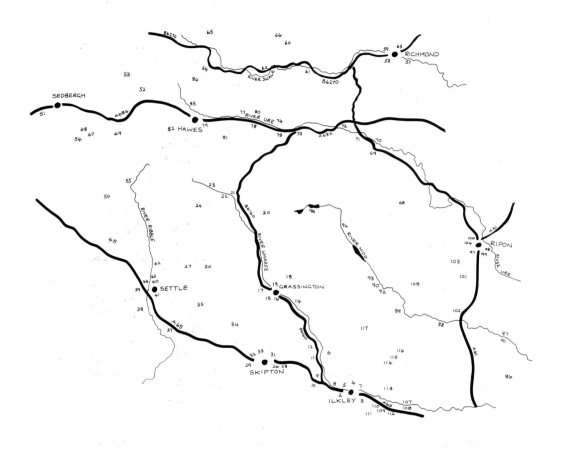

2.   Heathcote, Ilkley
3.   Cow and Calf rocks, Ilkley
4.   Roman wall, Ilkley
5.   Donkey Jackson's steps, Ilkley
6.   Beamsley Hospital
7.   memorial bath, Iikley
8.   Low Mill, Addingham
9.   the Rookery, Addingham
10.   Craven Heifer pub, Addingham
11.   Bolton Bridge
12.   Bolton Abbey aqueducts
14.   lych gate, Burnsall
15.   Fountaine Hospital
16.   beeboles, Linton
17.   Threshfield School
18.   leadmines, Grassington

Ilkley, Addingham and Bolton Abbey

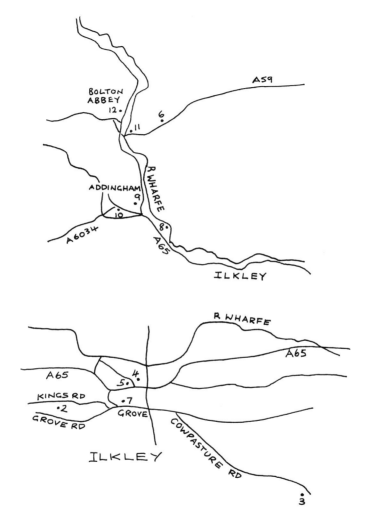

2. Heathcote, Ilkley
3. Cow and Calf rocks, Ilkley
4. Roman wall, Ilkley
5. Donkey Jackson's steps, Ilkley
6. Beamsley Hospital
7. memorial bath, Ilkley

8. Low Mill, Addingham
9. the Rookery, Addingham
10. Craven Heifer pub, Addingham
11. Bolton Bridge
12. Bolton Abbey aqueducts

A House of Fame

There are few buildings in and around the Dales which are known internationally. Heathcote in Ilkley is one of them. It was designed by Sir Edwin Lutyens (1869-1944), the great modern architect who used classical idioms in a very individual way. His greatest memorial will perhaps be the public buildings of New Delhi, but in England he created many grand villas and Heathcote is certainly the grandest of all Ilkley's villas. It was built in 1906 for a wealthy wool manufacturer called Hemingway and is now a headquarters building for an industrial concern.

Lutyens spared no expense in its construction. He designed everything from furniture to soft furnishings, from door handles and bell pulls to a graceful iron staircase. The fittings, together with his use of exotic marbles including a green Siberian marble used for the first time in England, make for a richly splendid interior.

The exterior, built with stone from Guiseley and Morley and a pantile roof, is one of bold blocks and massive chimneys, in a style derived from several sources but essentially one of Lutyens' own. It could happily sit with his New Delhi buildings and does not blend easily with most of Victorian and Edwardian Ilkley. It is magnificent nevertheless.

Site: About half a mile (1km) west of Ilkley town centre along Grove Road and Kings Road, and can be seen from either.

Grid Ref: SE 108476

The Cow and Calf

Everyone who knows Ilkley will know of the Cow and Calf rocks. Local belief has it that there was once a Bull rock too, much nearer to the road, which was used as a source of stone for some of Ilkley's buildings, in particular one of the hotels, but historians tell us that the Bull was fictitious.

No one knows the origin of the name, but legend has it that the calf was formed when Giant Rombald of Rombalds Moor was being chased by his wife. Striding across the valley to Almscliff Crag, his foot slipped, and in slipping he broke the calf from the cow. Meanwhile his wife dropped the stones she was throwing at him, and where she dropped them, a mile or so south on the moor, is still known as the 'Great Skirtful of Stones'.

The Cow and Calf quarry is now a practising ground for climbers and a place of assembly for occasional celebrations to sing *Ilkley Moor B'aht 'at* or for a service at dawn on Easter Sunday.

The rocks around make a superb viewpoint with views over much of Wharfedale. In them have been carved the initials or names of generations of visitors who have enjoyed the view.

Site: about a mile (1.5km) from Ilkley town centre up Cowpasture Road and Hanginggate Road.

Grid Ref: SE 131466

The Roman Wall

No, not Hadrian's Wall, merely a short length of wall behind the Manor House at Ilkley which, to the uninitiated, could be any old wall.

But it is Roman, dating from the third century, and it is the west wall of a fort which was first established in Ilkley about AD 80, the only visible remains of Roman occupation in its original position, though the Manor House Museum has a number of Roman exhibits found locally, including some fine tombstones.

The fort, rebuilt twice, and on the second occasion of stone rather than timber, held almost 500 soldiers, a quarter of them cavalry, together with the necessary barracks, stables, workshops, bathhouse and so on. With its neighbouring civil settlement it must have had a name. But what was it? Don't tell the people of Ilkley but the long accepted name of 'Olicana', after which many local organisations are named, may well have been elsewhere.

Site: behind the Manor House Museum which is off Church Street.
Grid Ref: SE 116479

Donkey Jackson's Steps

The bitterly cold waters of the plunge bath of White Wells on Ilkley Moor were once described as 'mellifluous, diaphanous, luminous, transparent, pellucid, immaculate and unequalled in purity'.

From the beginnings of Ilkley's fame as a spa in the early nineteenth century, several local entrepreneurs provided donkeys, with or without carriages, to transport those visitors who were unable or unwilling to walk up the moor for their total immersion in these chilling but reputedly health-giving waters. The donkey trade continued into the present century.

One of the donkey owners was John (Donkey) Jackson whose business was in Bridge Lane. He died in 1907 at the age of eighty-one, having worked until the previous year; a character who appears on numerous old photographs.

His cottage no longer exists but the steps which led to it are still there.

Site: Bridge Lane is the first turning to the right after leaving the centre of Ilkley in the Skipton direction on the A65.
Grid Ref: SE 115478

A Legacy of Lady Anne

Dales folk have many reasons to be grateful to Lady Anne Clifford, not least her restoration of Skipton Castle after the Civil War and the subsequent partial demolition. But in Beamsley Hospital she left us an absolutely delightful building. Founded by her mother in 1593, Lady Anne finished it off.

It was built for 13 widows, 12 of them to be called sisters and the thirteenth, the 'mother', to act as supervisor. Six of them lived in a two-storied range of cottages parallel to the main road, and the other six, with the 'mother', in seven apartments running round the circumference of a small circular building, at the centre of which was a chapel lit by a lantern.

In use until comparatively recently, the building is now owned by the Landmark Trust and let as holiday accommodation. It is a little gem.

Site: about 1,000 yards (900m) east of the bridge over the River Wharfe on the A59.
Grid Ref: SE 082531

A Bath for Vinzenz Priessnitz

In 1829 Vinzenz Priessnitz, a Silesian farmer, introduced to the world of the spas the idea that water, without any significant mineral content, could provide all kinds of cures so long as it was cold enough.

Bathing, soaking various parts of the body, wrapping in wet sheets and so on could work wonders provided you survived the treatment and did not freeze to death.

The system (hydropathy) was introduced to Ilkley by a merchant called Hamer Stansfield who set up a company to build the Ben Rhydding Hydro at a cost of £30,000. In the grounds of the hydro, opened in 1844, Stansfield erected a shrine or temple to Priessnitz which included a fountain. A bath which was part of the structure now stands in the Grove at Ilkley (pictured, with a detail of its end), inscribed to 'The Silesian peasant to whom the world is indebted for the blessing of the SYSTEM OF CURE BY COLD WATER'.

Site: in a small public garden on the north side of the Grove, Ilkley, about 200 yards (180m) from Brook Street.

Grid Ref: SE 115476

The Penny Hole

Low Mill at Addingham was by far the biggest mill in the town and 'the second oldest and first successful spinning mill in the world'.

It had a chequered history, the most dramatic episode being at the time of the Luddites, when groups of workmen roamed the country wrecking the machinery they believed would throw them out of work. In 1826 a mob from both Lancashire and the nearby parts of Yorkshire, flushed with success at having turned back a consignment of spinning mules destined for Low Mill, were advancing on the mill itself. The workpeople and their wives prepared to defend themselves with stones from the river to use as missiles, placing grilles over windows and collecting firearms. In the event, the Riot Act was read, soldiers called in and the rioters driven away, but not before one who had been trying to climb a roof drowned when he fell into the open tank from the privies.

Now all is peaceful. The mill premises have been converted into houses, and names like 'Counting House' and 'Weighbridge' recall the various parts of the mill. The most intriguing is 'Penny Hole' where workers clocked in and paid a penny fine if they were late.

Site: turn right on a minor road from the A65 about two miles (3km) from Ilkley: then right again.

Grid Ref: SE 091494

The Rookery

The rookery at Addingham was built at the beginning of the nineteenth century. It consisted of two rows of back-to-back houses with a loom shop at one end running at right angles to them. Part of this seems to have been used as living accommodation at the time of the mid-century censuses.

In 1841 a total of 80 people lived there; 26 men all working, 25 women of whom 20 worked, and 29 children under 11 not working. Of the 40 people working, 39 were in textiles, 10 of whom were in cotton and 29 in wool/worsted.

By 1851 there was a small reduction in numbers, but in one of these tiny two-room houses there was an Isaac Morrison, dealer in pots, with his wife and three children, together with Jacob Miller, dealer in pots and old iron, with his wife and six children. Thirteen people in all.

The good old days.

Site: about 200 yards (180m) from Addingham Main Street along Bolton Road.
Grid Ref: SE 078498

The Craven Heifer

Bred at Bolton Abbey by the Rev William Carr at the beginning of the nineteenth century, the Craven Heifer attained such an enormous size that a subsequent owner exhibited it widely at fairs and shows. Its dimensions were 10 ft 2 ins (3.1m) in girth, 9 ft 11 ins (3m) round the loin, 11 ft 2 ins (3.4m) from nose to rump and 5 ft 2 ins (1.6m) high at the shoulder. It is said that its weight never stopped increasing. Sadly its fate was settled at a cock fight. A man from Huddersfield won the animal, only to sell her off at one shilling a pound. Her weight then was 2,400 lbs (1,090kg).

Though the end was sad, the memory lingered for a while at the Craven Bank whose notes carried a picture of the heifer and, more lastingly, in the names of several inns in the area.

Whisper it not to the man from Bolton Abbey, but the Airedale Heifer was bigger.

Site: at the junction of the Skipton and Silsden roads in Addingham.
Grid Ref: SE 072499

A Bridge Too Many?

An ancient route from Cheshire and Lancashire into Yorkshire goes by Skipton, Bolton Abbey and Blubberhouses and continues to Knaresborough and York. The crossing of the Wharfe at Bolton Abbey must always have been a problem. A bridge is known to have existed there in 1318 and again in the sixteenth century. It is also known that a flood destroyed the bridge on 17th September 1673, when many other bridges up and down the Wharfe were also washed away. It is quite likely that for long periods before then there was no bridge and travellers had to rely on a ford.

It is the kind of place where a hermit would live, helping travellers across the river or keeping the bridge, if any, in repair. Bridge or no bridge, crossing might at times be dangerous, and travellers were reminded of this by an inscription on a beam in a cottage at one side of the river which reads:
'Thou that passeth by this way
One Ave Maria here thou'll say.'
In recent years the replacement bridge which followed the 1673 flood was declared unsafe and has been bypassed by yet another bridge. Fortunately the old one remains; with little traffic, it should be with us for many more centuries.

Site: a few hundred yards from the Devonshire Arms at Bolton Abbey on the old Blubberhouses road.
Grid Ref: SE 072522

The Aqueducts of Bolton Abbey

There are two aqueducts at Bolton Abbey, both of them unrecognised for what they are, at least by many. One is relatively modern, a little way downstream from Barden Bridge. Though designed with small turrets and castellation to add interest to the landscape, it does in fact hide a pipeline carrying drinking water from the Dales.

The second aqueduct is seen by every motorist, cursed by some, but admired by all. It is a three-arched structure, mediaeval in origin, straddling the road close to a hall which was added to the great gateway of the abbey for use as a shooting lodge. King George V stayed there on several occasions.

The aqueduct provided power for a corn mill on the abbey side of the road. On the other side, a few hundred yards up a public footpath, can be seen the dams which supplied the water.

Site: on the B1660 just north of Bolton Abbey village.

Grid Ref: SE 072541

The Wharfe Valley

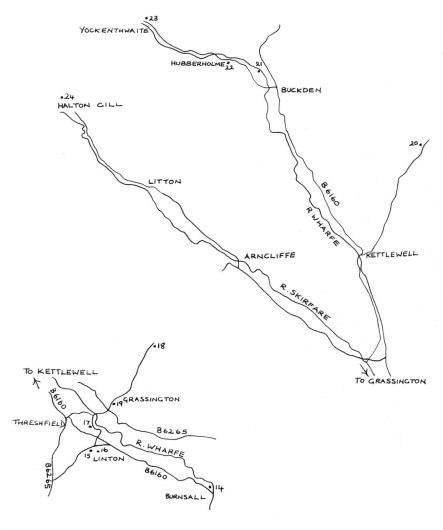

14. lych gate, Burnsall
15. Fountaine Hospital
16. beeboles, Linton
17. Threshfield School
18. leadmines, Grassington
19. Grasssington Theatre

20. Tor Dyke
21. stone trap, River Wharfe
22. 'Parliament', Hubberholme
23. Yockenthwaite stone circle
24. Miles Wilson

An Extraordinary Gate

Lych gates (corpse gates) are commonly found at the entrance to churchyards, often with a gabled roof. Many are Victorian.

At one time, before coffins came into general use, the shrouded corpse would be carried to the gate and the first part of the funeral service read there.

The gate at Burnsall is of rare design. It is equipped with ropes and pulleys which enable it to swing on a central pivot. Though reconstructed, it is the same as an earlier gate which may have been first built in the seventeenth century.

The church itself is undoubtedly very ancient and may well have its origins in a visit by St Wilfrid in the seventh century. It has some remains of Anglo-Saxon crosses, Viking hog-back tombstones, a Norman tub front, a fifteenth century alabaster panel and a fine Jacobean pulpit.

Outside in the graveyard is a tombstone designed and carved by the sculptor Eric Gill in 1934 for members of the Dawson family, lords of the manor of Hartlington.

Site: Burnsall is on the B6160, six miles (9.5km) north-west of Bolton Abbey.
Grid Ref: SE 032615

A Monumental Almshouse

Linton, village of three bridges, of Linton Hall and other seventeenth century houses, and said — rightly in my view — to be one of the most beautiful villages in Yorkshire, is dominated by an extraordinary building, Fountaine Hospital. In some ways quite incongruous, it nevertheless provides an extremely impressive background to the much-photographed village green. It is said that no less a person than Vanbrugh himself may have been the architect.

It was founded in 1721, financed by bequests under the will of Richard Fountaine, a member of a local family who went to London and became very wealthy. The hospital, an almshouse, was planned to house six poor men or women, for whom a further bequest of £26 per annum was to provide a coat or gown 'Blew lined with green'.

The hospital still flourishes as an almshouse, its roof, dome and chapel recently completely refurbished.

Site: from the B6265 north of Skipton, branch right near to Swinden quarry for Linton village.

Grid Ref: SD 997627

Bees in their Boles

Before sugar was cheap and easily available, beekeeping was common in the Dales. The hives were of the old-fashioned kind, made of straw or wicker work or even, in the Dales, of ling. They were kept in recesses in walls, called boles, and these

recesses can be widely seen. Although variable in shape, they are typically about two feet square and eighteen inches deep, and mostly face south.

Beehives in the modern style came into use about 1860, so beeboles will usually be older than that and some may be centuries old. The most impressive array, carefully restored, is at Nutwith Cote near Masham, formerly a grange of Fountains Abbey, but there are much larger numbers to be seen in a garden at West Scrafton, and the largest number of all is in a range behind Stainforth Youth Hostel but they are in a sad state of disrepair.

These pictured here are at Linton.

Site: from Linton village, cross the clapper bridge and walk for about 100 yards (90m) on the footpath to Thorpe.

Grid Ref: SD 998626

At School in the Dales

The Dales had many fine grammar schools. One such is at Threshfield where the original 1674 building is still in use as a school.

Founded by the Rev Matthew Hewitt, a rector of the parish and a member of a local family, it produced some remarkable results. Old boys included Dr T D Whitaker, author of *The History of Craven*, Dr Dodgson, later a bishop, and Dr W Craven, later master of St John's College, Cambridge. During the period 1715 to 1732 no less than twenty-one boys went from the school to Cambridge.

Just as remarkable as its successes were its punishments. One was to stand on one leg and hold a heavy log with the arm at full stretch, the log having written on it a passage which had to be learned by heart before the punishment ended. Another, after being caught stealing fruit or berries, was to sew them back on the trees with needle and thread.

Site: from the B6265, turn right just before Grassington Bridge. The school is about 500 yards (450m) on the right.

Grid Ref: SD 998634

The Grassington Mines

Grassington was one of the main leadmining areas of the Dales. Mining probably began centuries earlier, but it was the Earl of Cumberland who first developed the field in 1603 by bringing men from his mines in Derbyshire, and it was the Duke of Devonshire in the eighteenth century who continued that development and created a flourishing industry.

He built a new smelt mill and a water course (the Duke's Level) which drained a huge area and made deeper mining possible. Many remains of the leadmining age can be seen above Grassington. The mill manager's house is there, the former blacksmith's shop, a powder house (for explosives) and an entrance dated 1828 to one of the working levels. Nearby are bell pits — evidence of early, primitive mining methods — while a little further away but easily accessible are the bouse teams

where ore was stored, the remains of an ore-crushing plant and a deep shaft. Somewhat further away is the smelt mill, the long flue and its chimney.

All have explanatory notices — or did have until vandals did their worst.

Site: about two miles (3km) north of Grassington on Moor Lane, to the limit of the metalled road.

Grid Ref: SE 017659

The National Theatre of the Dales

Tom Airey, born in 1771, carrier and post-master, must have been a remarkable man. Having performed in many a drama at school, his zest for the theatre was fired by the visit of a touring company with Edmund Kean to a theatre at Skipton in the yard of the Hole in the Wall Inn.

There Tom discovered Shakespeare, appeared in *Richard III* and resolved to form his own company at Grassington. He succeeded, for many years using a barn in Garrs Lane, now a private house (Theatre Cottage).

He attracted some of the leading lights of Kean's company, including Kean himself and Miss Harriet Mellon, later the Duchess of St Albans.

The venture collapsed sometime in the 1830s. Even if Edmund Bogg is accurate in suggesting that 'A hoss, a hoss, wh'ull hev me kindum for a hoss' was typical of Tom, at least he brought Shakespeare and drama of all kinds to what was then a small, largely industrial, town. Tom died in 1842 at the age of seventy-one.

Site: 100 yards (90m) from Grassington square.
Grid Ref: SE 003641

An Archaeological Puzzle

The Dales are full of archaeological riches, many of them not easily accessible. But Tor Dyke is easily seen and visited. It is a huge earthwork. The writer Edmund Bogg said of it:

'For 2½ miles runs a deep trench, in many places yet 12 to 14 feet deep ... the entrenchment would shelter an army of several thousands ... its defensive properties can easily be grasped ... we should imagine that the barrier has been made by the early British to stem the tide of Roman invasion.'

It is not 2½ miles (4km) long but it is certainly most impressive. In other parts of England it would be a major tourist attraction.

But there is in fact no hard evidence that it was built by the Brigantes as defence against the Romans. It probably was, but its date is uncertain. See what you think.

Site: the eastern end is about 2 miles (3km) north of Kettlewell on the road into Coverdale.

Grid Ref: SD 986757

A Stone Trap

Did you ever hear of anyone setting a trap for stones? Well they have, and you can see one in upper Wharfedale by taking a short riverside walk between Hubberholme and Buckden.

When the Wharfe is in spate after heavy rain the power of the rushing water is immense, and huge stones can be carried downstream as if they were little more than grains of sand. They may then accumulate in inconvenient places or, worse, do a great deal of damage to the riverbank or riverside structures.

If you can substantially reduce the speed of flow, the river no longer has the power to carry large stones and they will be deposited on its bed. One simple way of doing this is to dig a deep hole in the riverbed so that the depth at that point is much greater than elsewhere and the flow correspondingly calm.

You have then made a stone trap, but don't forget to clear it out from time to time.

Site: the trap can be approached from the minor road (Dubb's Lane) leading from Buckden to Hubberholme; walk along the Dales Way for about 300 yards (275m).
Grid Ref: NY 935780

A Parliament at Hubberholme

Hubberholme has a marvellous little church, with one of only two rood lofts in the whole of Yorkshire and a plaque to J B Priestley, who thought it the most peaceful spot on earth and whose ashes lie in the graveyard. The rood loft was built in 1558, a remarkable survival.

But Hubberholme is also famous for its Parliament, a New Year's Eve gathering in the George Inn to let land (the 'Poor Pasture') for the benefit of the poor. Traditionally the vicar and the churchwardens constitute the 'House of Lords' and local farmers the 'House of Commons'.

The vicar attends the Commons and conducts a candle auction, an ancient custom in which the auction has to be concluded by the time an ordinary household candle splutters its last light. It is a festive occasion whose origins are unknown but may have begun about 200 years ago.

Of one vicar it is recorded that the farmers liked to ply him with drink because 'he became merry without very much of it' and would then sing a popular song of the day: 'Tottie will you go, Tottie will you go, down to the banks of the Ohio'.

Oh to have been there!

Site: five miles (8km) north of Kettlewell on the road to Hawes.
Grid Ref: SD 926783

The Prehistoric Dalesman

From the Stone Age, man has lived in the Dales. Artefacts from various caves, the best known of which is Victoria Cave near Settle where a harpoon and carvings were found, are clear evidence of Stone Age occupation. Elsewhere flints, stone axes and cave burials have been found, and in Penyghent Gill there is the so-called Giants Grave, a stone burial chamber underneath a substantial earth mound.

The Bronze Age left much more evidence in the shape of tools, pottery and ornaments. On the ground, evidence such as that of Ilkley Moor with its cup and ring marked rocks and other mysterious carvings are quite common, and there are several stone circles including the Twelve Apostles, also high on Ilkley Moor.

Unfortunately there is little that is very easily accessible. One of the easiest among these signs of prehistoric man is a small stone circle, probably marking a burial place, near the hamlet of Yockenthwaite. Another is a henge (a central

circular platform with a ditch and bank) at Yarnbury, where late Stone Age or early Bronze Age man would meet for some ritual ceremony.

Site: Stone circle — 200 yards (180m) upriver long the Dales Way from the bridge at Yockenthwaite, which is seven miles (11km) north-west of Kettlewell on the Hawes road. Henge — just over a mile (1.5km) north of Grassington on Moor Lane, a footpath veers off to the right to pass the henge just before the next wall.

Grid Ref: stone circle — SD 904792; henge — SE 014654

The Sci-Fi Author of Littondale

Miles Wilson was curate of Halton Gill from 1737 until his death in 1776, a very long time. Clearly he liked being there and his parishioners were probably well suited with him, but he was certainly an eccentric, giving much time to his own pursuits.

He is said to have had a genius for mechanical work and to have constructed a weather glass, a representation of an ape blowing a trumpet and an 'oracular' head, whatever that might have been. He could also read the future.

His most extraordinary achievement was to write *The Man in the Moon* about a cobbler who went to the top of Penyghent, then climbed to the moon. From there he made a tour of the solar system, during the course of which he discovered that the inhabitants of one of the planets were made of pot metal.

Dr Whitaker said of him: 'a man of talents ... had he been blessed with a sound mind and a superior education, he would have been capable of much better things'.

Pictured is the former Chapel of St John in Halton Gill.

Site: approximately eight miles (13km) up Littondale from the junction with the Skipton-Kettlewell road.

Grid Ref: SD 880766

Skipton and Airedale

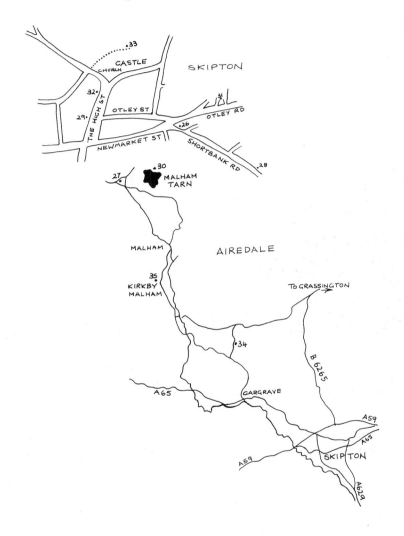

26. Skipton Grammar School
27. globe flower and
    birdseye primrose
28. Shortbank Road, Skipton
29. old town hall, Skipton
30. Walter Morrison

31. King St, Skipton
32. Black Horse, Skipton
33. Skipton Castle
34. Friars Head
35. grave, Kirkby Malham Church

The Old Grammar School

The grammar school at Skipton, founded in 1548 by William Ermysted, Canon Residentiary of St Paul's, was really a refoundation of a chantry school which had existed since at least 1492.

Pupils had to attend from 6am to 6pm in summer with two hours less in winter. As well as teaching English, the headmaster, who was to be called the 'Pedagogue of the Pedagogy', had to make frequent use of Latin, 'exacting from the more advanced scholars that they compose Epistles, Orations and Verses, explaining to the same their Scholars, the Authors promoting thereto, to wit, Virgil, Terence, Ovid and other Poets'.

The school was in Ermysted's house which had formerly been a chapel of the Knights Hospitallers. It consisted basically of only one room with an adjoining school house which was rebuilt in about 1773. It is now an electricity sub-station, the school having moved to new premises in 1871.

Incidentally, John Wesley had hopes of the headship in 1727 but in the end he was not nominated. That was probably just as well because he had come to the conclusion that Skipton was a 'frightful' place where there would be no society in which he would be at ease.

Site: Leave Skipton town centre by Newmarket Street and go straight ahead at a mini-roundabout. The old school is set back on the left about 200 yards (180m) further on.
Grid Ref: SD 994517

Two Very Special Flowers of the Dales

The limestone Dales provide superb habitats for wild flowers and, as every year passes, increasing numbers can be seen in the upper dales where farmers no longer take silage crops but make hay by traditional methods.

Some of the flowers, such as purple saxifrage which grows on the high cliffs of Penyghent, are almost inaccessible. Others such as mountain pansy, rockrose and thrift mostly require a fair walk to see them, but many more such as primrose, bluebell, king-cup, monkey flower, some of the cranesbills and giant bellflower can easily be seen, often without leaving the car.

Two of my favourite flowers, which are spec-ialities of the Dales, are birds-eye primrose and globe flower. The first (below) can be seen along the roadside in Langstrothdale, but the globe flower (above) is much more elusive. The best place is a tiny reserve called Globe Flower Wood near Mal-ham. You can't go in but you can see over the wall.

Site: turn left at the first crossroads on the Malham to Arncliffe road; the wood is at the next junction.

Grid Ref: SD 873667

'The steepest hill I ever saw'

Shortbank (formerly Shodebank) Road at Skipton leads to Rombalds Moor and so to the route of the old Roman road to Ilkley. It was in Shortbank Road that a Dr Dodgson developed a bath and pleasure garden in the 1840s, but the venture was not a commercial success and Skipton's life as a spa town soon came to an end.

Near to where Dr Dodgson built his baths was a toll house which still exists. Paying a toll must indeed have added insult to injury, for travelling this road was no

doubt an unpleasant experience. The poet Gray called it 'The steepest hill I ever saw a road carried over in England'. A slight exaggeration, perhaps, but the construction of a new road through Draughton in the middle of the eighteenth century would certainly have been greeted with relief.

You should go past the toll house to the limit of the metalled road if you wish to see the beginning of the steepest part of the road which Gray found so daunting.

Site: leave Skipton town centre by Newmarket Street and go straight ahead at a mini-roundabout into Shortbank Road.

Grid Ref: SD 999514

Skipton's Old Town Hall

Recently given a facelift and a new role as a tourist information centre, the old town hall at Skipton has been rescued from the obscurity of only a few years ago, an obscurity which did no justice to its history.

With beginnings in the seventeenth century when it was built by Lady Anne Clifford, it was town hall, tollbooth and courthouse until the new town hall was built in 1862. The general Quarter Sessions for the Peace for the West Riding were also held there once a year. In addition it served as a local lock-up for men.

At each side of the rather grand flight of steps is a part of the stocks of old Skipton. They and a whipping post had previously stood near to the market cross at the other side of the High Street. The other main instrument of punishment, the ducking stool, was near the canal bridge in what is now Coach Street.

Site: on the west side of Middle Row, a range of buildings in the High Street.
Grid Ref: SD 990517

The Water Babies

Walter Morrison MP, pipe smoker, walker, multi-millionaire and philanthropist, had a home in Malham Tarn House for over sixty years. He had been educated at Eton and Balliol, and from business ventures in textiles and in South America he managed to increase his family's already immense wealth.

But he was a modest man, despising public honours, who would think nothing of walking home from Settle Station after returning from business in London. He spent money carefully, but was generous with local benefactions.

A number of eminent Victorians were entertained by Morrison at Malham, including Ruskin and Charles Kingsley. Kingsley arrived intending to write about the Rising of the North in 1569. Instead, inspired by Malham Cove and other local places, especially Arncliffe, he wrote *The Water Babies*.

Site: leave Malham village on the Arncliffe road and turn right for the tarn. The house is the other side of the water; a footpath goes by it.

Grid Ref: SD 894672

A Bit of Building Society History

In the early days of building societies they were not 'permanent' but 'terminating'. They were designed to be liquidated as soon as their purpose was complete, their purpose normally being to build houses for the individuals who formed the society. Typically these individuals would club together (hence the popularity of the name 'Club Houses') to build a row of houses, often on a DIY basis, and then perhaps draw lots to decide the order of occupation when they were finished.

One such society was the Skipton Tradesman's Building Society which was established in 1823. It built fifty-four houses in Commercial Street, which have since been demolished. The members, thirty-nine of them, were all skilled tradesmen or people of some financial standing. In the event, few lived in the houses on completion and for many the venture must have been a speculative one from the outset.

King Street (pictured) and Queen Street were built by the Hart's Head Building Society which existed from 1825 to 1840.

Site: approximately half a mile (0.8km) from Skipton town centre on the Otley road (A6069). Grid Ref: SD 997518

The Old Inns of Skipton

There is no shortage of inns in Skipton, though the high numbers of the late nineteenth century are now much reduced. Happily some of the more ancient establishments remain, and of these the Red Lion and the Black Horse on opposite sides of the High Street are possibly the most interesting.

The Red Lion is said to have been built on the site of St Mary Magdalene, a leper hospital of 1310-1350 and, despite being rebuilt on several occasions, some of the existing woodwork dates from the fourteenth century.

The Black Horse building is younger, dating from 1676. It

is reputed to be on the site of the royal mews of Richard III when he held the Honour of Skipton late in the fifteenth century. It was once known as the Kings Head.

Site: the Black Horse is at the top end of Skipton High Street, on the left as you face the church; the Red Lion is on the other side.

Grid Ref: SD 990518

Behind the Castle

All visitors to Skipton see the great gateway of the castle, but few go round to look at its back. It is well worth going for three reasons.

First to see the almost vertical rock-face on which the castle sits and to appreciate its near-invincible position. Second to imagine the scene without the canal when the area was the pleasure garden of the mediaeval castle in which the ladies took the air, dallied and no doubt flirted. Thirdly to look at the canal itself, the Springs Canal, constructed in the late eighteenth century to carry stone from Haw Bank Quarry at Embsay. By the second half of the nineteenth century, locomotives hauled stone-filled wagons to the top of an incline behind the castle. They were then lowered by wire rope to a point where their contents could be dropped down chutes into waiting barges, which were then hauled to the main Leeds-Liverpool Canal. Mule-power and, sometimes, man-power was used. The remains of the chutes can still be seen at the far end of the canal.

Site: reached by canal-side footpath which is accessed from Mill Bridge.
Grid Ref: SD 992521

My Favourite Dales Building

Friars Head, a little-known jewel, is my favourite Dales building. In its setting it is stunning, with its almost symmetrical façade topped by a collection of delicate finials. Below them, in the apex of the gables, are windows with three lights and an unusual ogee shape and, below them again, is a superb array of mullioned and transomed bay windows.

It was built about the very end of the sixteenth century by Stephen Proctor, who had made money out of lead and iron. He is said to have invented a family tree and to have bought his knighthood in 1604.

Later, he went on to build Fountains Hall (right). Even though his methods may not have been the most honourable, we must be thankful that he left behind two such beautiful buildings.

Site: from the Gargrave to Malham road, about two miles (3km) from Gargrave, turn right towards Winterburn.

Grid Ref: SD 932575

A Watery Grave

As its name implies, Kirkby Malham has a long church history, but its present building owes much to the monks at the abbey of West Dereham in Norfolk who seem to have intended it as a monastic church. Its size is much larger than the local population can ever have justified. It is a church with many interesting features, including some old family pews and Georgian box pews.

Outside in the graveyard is a very odd grave. The wife of Colonel John Frederick Harrison, a sea captain often in the distant oceans of the world, vowed that death would not unite them and that they were to be buried on each side of a small stream. 'As water parted us in life, so it shall in death.'

It was not to be. The ground was too rocky and she had to be buried above her husband.

The memorial remains, straddling a stream.

Site: five miles (8km) north of Gargrave on the road to Malham.

Grid Ref: SD 894610

Settle Area

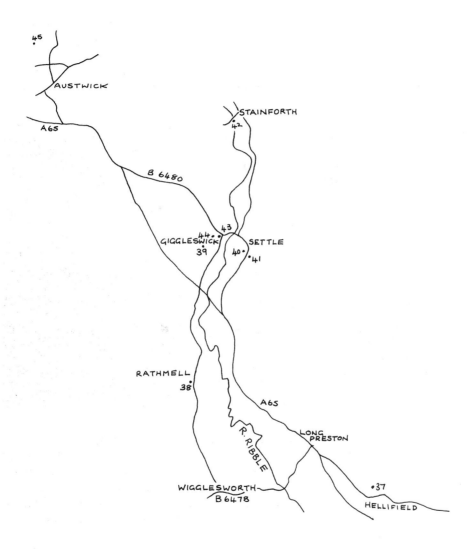

37. Hellifield Station
38. College Fold, Rathmell
39. Giggleswick Chapel
40. Naked Man, Settle
41. the Folly, Settle

42. Stainforth Bridge
43. Edward Elgar & Dr Buck
44. lintels, Giggleswick
45. Norber erratics

Settle–Carlisle

The very phrase 'Settle–Carlisle' has a romantic and dramatic ring about it. Pictures, real or imagined, of steam locomotives at the limit of their power climbing the gradients of this famous railway line in the snowy depths of winter, visions of the wild countryside through which it goes, or admiration of those who fought so long to save the line from closure, are all part of the romance of 'Settle–Carlisle'.

Hellifield railway station is a small but important part of the picture. First opened on the 1st June 1880 by the Midland Railway, it was scheduled as a Grade II listed building but by the early 1990s it was in a very sorry state. Once the line had been saved it was clear that the station had to be refurbished. British Rail, English Heritage, the Rural Development Commission, Craven Council, the Settle Carlisle Railway Trust and the Railway Heritage Club all provided funds. Its superb Victorian cast iron canopy is once again in mint condition.

With hopes of constructing a heritage centre, hotel and golf course at Hellifield, it may be that the station will have a future as grand as its past.

Site: a few hundred yards north of the A65 at Hellifield.
Grid Ref: SD 852672

Dissension in Rathmell

The Rev Richard Frankland was born in Rathmell in 1630. Educated at Giggleswick and Cambridge, he became a professor at Durham and held the living at Bishop Auckland. Along with many other parish priests, he resigned when he could not give his 'unfeigned consent and assent' to everything contained in the revised Prayer Book as required by the Act of Uniformity of 1662.

Persecution of dissenters was at its height when Frankland established the first nonconformist college in England at what is now a private residence known as College Fold, Rathmell. Repressed four years later, the academy was compelled to live a wandering existence, for part of the time having its home in Calton Hall, Malhamdale.

Following the Act of Toleration in 1689, it returned to Rathmell where Frankland died nine years later. During his lifetime he had trained no less than 304 students for the dissenting ministry. A man of considerable courage, he once had the temerity to beg King Charles to reform his life.

Site: approximately three miles (5km) south of Settle on the Wigglesworth road.
Grid Ref: SD 804601

Giggleswick Chapel

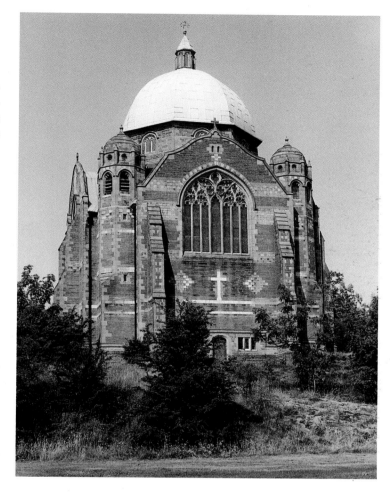

The great green copper dome of Giggleswick school chapel is a landmark for miles around.

Built between 1897 and 1901 on a mound of rock, its situation is truly dominant and the view from it up Ribblesdale quite remarkable. It was the gift of Walter Morrison of Malham Tarn House at a cost of over £50,000, who insisted that the chapel had a dome such as he had seen in mosques. The architect, Sir Thomas Jackson, delighted at a chance given to few in his profession, was determined to show that domes and Gothic architecture are not incompatible, despite shocking the purists.

He thought he succeeded and few would disagree. It is a majestic building. Its interior — with rich mosaic work, representations of angels and figures of the evangelists — is sheer Victorian exuberance. It is not usually open to the general public, but many events — musical concerts and the like — are held there.

Curiously, when you are in the middle of Giggleswick — that most charming of villages — the chapel is impossible to see and not easy to locate. But it is certainly worth the effort.

Site: off a steep lane going west out of Giggleswick village.
Grid Ref: SD 807639

Naked in Settle

The 'naked man' of Settle simply has to be included in this collection. Surveying the market places, as he does, he is said to have been covered up for fear of offending Queen Victoria, though at first sight he appears to achieve a certain modesty by holding a date plaque in front of him. Apart from the date (1663) it is not clear what he is holding, though it has been suggested that it is a carpenter's plane and that the figure itself is the trade sign of a carpenter.

What is clear, however, is that the man is not naked; his jacket, breeches and hose are clearly visible. It is also known that the Naked Man was originally an inn.

In Langcliffe he has a partner. High in the gable of a house is a so-called 'naked woman'.

Site: in Settle Market Square, at the Naked Man Café.

Grid Ref: SD 819637

A Folly to be Proud of

If you did not know it was there, you would be astonished to find a seventeenth century house of such size and extravagance in the middle of a small town. It was in a rather more open situation when Richard Preston built it overlooking his estates in 1679. Originally it was called Tanner Hall, but has long been dubbed 'The Folly', perhaps because Preston became bankrupt due to high building costs but more likely because of its very downmarket later use for everything from scrap-metal dealing to selling fish and chips. Fortunately its recent owners had more respect for the building and restored it, and its future is likely to be as a heritage museum. The interior is open to the public.

Whatever the origin of its name, I like to think that it can be attributed to its architectural features — the fantastic main entrance, the magnificent mullioned windows which go round corners, the huge fireplace and the mediaeval-style tower which houses the main staircase. And much more.

Site: 100 yards (90m) from Settle Market Place.

Grid Ref: SD 821636

Sunbathing and Salmon

Stainforth's single-arch bridge is one of the finest in the Dales. The name indicates that a ford existed here, and it is not known when a bridge was first erected, though one might have been built in the four-teenth century by the monks of Sawley Abbey. The present structure is said to date from about 1675, and the prob-ability is that it was built by Samuel Watson as an easy access to the main Ribblesdale road from his house at Knight Stainforth Hall, built about 1670. The walled lane from the bridge leads past the hall.

The river just below the bridge is one of the honeypots of the Dales on a hot summer day, a perfect place for children to play and all to enjoy the sun; it can seem as crowded as Blackpool beach. A little further down is a deep pool into which the more adventurous can jump or dive from a considerable height, and close by is Stainforth Force (or Foss). When conditions are right in late summer it is one of the best places to watch salmon leaping.

Site: down a very narrow lane leaving the B6470 about two miles (3km) north of Settle. Grid Ref: SD 818673

The Elgar Connection

Charles William Buck was a doctor in Settle. He was also a keen amateur musician, involved in all kinds of music-making. While at a conference in Worcester in 1882 he was invited to play in an orchestra at a musical evening. A certain Edward Elgar, then little-known, was the conductor.

The two men became friends, and Elgar was introduced to the footpaths and fields of the Settle area while on a visit to Dr Buck. Both men loved walking, and in succeeding visits they built up a network of favourite routes and favourite places. The Elgar Way, a walk recently devised by W R Mitchell, links many of the places they visited.

While in the area Elgar stayed at Cravendale, Dr Buck's house in Giggleswick. What a pity that while staying there Elgar did not write music about the Dales as majestic as that which he wrote about the Malvern Hills. Even so there is no doubt that the Dales inspired him.

Site: just off the A65 in the middle of Giggleswick village, which is half a mile (0.8km) west of Settle.

Grid Ref: SD 813641

The Story of the Lintels

There can be no place in England which has more attractive carved stone door-lintels than the Yorkshire Dales. You see them everywhere. Many are quite restrained, merely carrying initials and dates; others are much more flamboyant.

The dates probably show when the house was built, but it is well to be cautious about them because lintels were sometimes taken out of an older house to be incorporated in a new one. Conversely the date may be that of an addition, perhaps a porch, to an older house.

The initials, often three of them, would

normally represent the surname of the builder and the first names of himself and his wife. A well-known example is Church House, Grassington (above), where the lintel, decorated with inverted hearts, is dated 1694 and has initials ASP for Stephen and Alice Peart.

Some lintels, like the one with a crudely carved bird at Kettlewell (above), are very simple, but the most flamboyant examples are to be found in Ribblesdale. Giggleswick is probably the best place to go to see a fine collection; that pictured on the right being just one of them.

Site: just off the A65 in the middle of Giggleswick village, which is about half a mile (0.8km) west of Settle.

Grid Ref: SD 812641

Erratic at Norber

Ice Age glaciers did much to shape the Dales, gouging out valleys, shaping smooth, rounded hills known as drumlins in Wharfedale and Ribblesdale, and leaving behind debris in lateral and terminal moraines such as that which dams up Malham Tarn.

Among minor glacial remains are the erratics, boulders of silurian gritstone which were carried and dropped by the ice a long way from their native land. At Norber such stranded rocks are perched on pedestals of limestone. The surrounding limestone has been dissolved by millenia of rainfall but the erratics, acting like umbrellas, have protected the limestone beneath them.

Glaciers left the Dales about 10,000 years ago, so the height of the pedestals indicate the rate the surrounding limestone has been dissolved: about an inch (2.5cm) every 1,000 years.

Site: a short walk from Crummack Lane which leaves Austwick to the north.
Grid Ref: SD 770698

The Far North-West

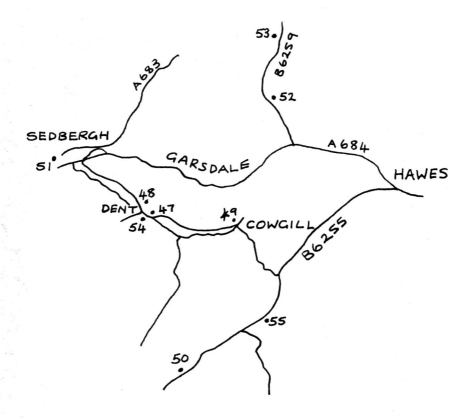

47. gravestone, Dent Church
48. High Hall, Dentdale
49. road sign, Dentdale
50. memorial, Chapel-le-Dale Church
51. Briggflatts Meeting House
52. Ais Gill Summit
53. Pendragon Castle
54. Sedgwick memorial, Dent
55. Gearstones

The Vampire of Dent

Have you ever heard of a vampire called George Hodgson?

In fact George lived in Dent and was well into his nineties before he died in 1715, but long before that his remarkable fitness in old age had been attributed to a deal with the Devil, and it was said that the shape of his teeth proved that he was a vampire.

Mysterious deaths of people claiming to have seen George after his burial led to exhumation and re-burial at the church porch with a stake through his heart.

His gravestone certainly has a hole in the appropriate place, but along with others I am inclined to take the view that the stone is merely a re-used gatepost. I have seen one of similar stone and with an exactly similar hole in a gate on the road from Dent through Deepdale.

Perhaps George can be given a posthumous pardon.

Site: Dent is six miles (9.5km) south-west of Sedburgh; the church is in its centre.
Grid Ref: SD 705871

Wuthering Heights, Dent?

High Hall, Dentdale, is a large farmhouse built in 1625 to replace an earlier house and extended in 1665. Architecturally it is remarkable for two reasons. First is a massive external chimney stack, while the second is the shape and style of the chimneys themselves. Large and round, they are such as you might expect to find in the Lake District and there are few like them in the Dales.

But that is not all that is of interest about High Hall. The Sill family who owned it were much involved in the slave trade and there were indeed slaves in Dent. Members of the family were part owners of slaving vessels (one was called the *Dent*) and had imported slaves to Dentdale as early as 1758.

It is said that the Brontës knew of the family and their activities. Parallels between them and Emily Brontë's famous story and even more famous characters has led some to believe that High Hall was a model for *Wuthering Heights*.

It is now open to the public as a centre for the preservation of rare breeds of farm animals.

Site: about half a mile (0.8km) north of Dent; off a minor road running on the north side of the river.

Grid Ref: SD 703876

Where Am I?

Direction stones and posts, or signposts as we now call them, were introduced in the seventeenth century and erected at crossroads. In 1697 they were made compulsory, but the law was not enforced and had to be reinforced by the Turnpike Acts of 1766 and 1773.

Mileposts, too, had to be provided along turnpikes and many of them still exist, some in stone, some iron, some flat, some triangular. Signposts also exist in a variety of designs and materials, ranging from stones with crudely-carved hands with fingers pointing the direction, to vast hoardings in the latest fashions of colour and lettering.

Examples of all of them can can found in the Dales. Among the rarities are the metal posts with a flat ring on top which actually gave you the map reference of where you were, as well as indicating the direction you needed to go. There are not many left.

Site: turn right for Cowgill from the B6255 about seven miles (11km) south-west of Hawes.

Grid Ref: SD 761869

Remembered in Chapel-le-Dale

High in the Dales in a valley below Whernside sits the tiny church of St Leonard of Chapel-le-Dale. Originally a chapel of ease for Ingleton and totally rebuilt in the seventeenth century, it was restored in 1869 when it was 'beautified at the cost of £500'. At that time, average annual interments had been two only. Unfortunately there was soon to be a deluge.

Navvies working on the Settle-Carlisle railway between 1869 and 1875 not only had extremely difficult work in terrible terrain and weather conditions, but also had appalling living conditions in which disease was rife. No less than 108 died building the viaduct at Ribblehead.

Many died and were buried on the open moorland, but Chapel-le-Dale graveyard was the final resting place for about 100 of them. They are commemorated by a tablet set up in 1876 by the Midland Railway Company and their fellow workmen.

Site: just off the B6255 from Ingleton to Hawes.

Grid Ref: SD 738772

The Peace of Briggflatts

George Fox spent ten years travelling the country questioning the preaching of the Church, and seeking a true faith to which he and every man could respond. He found it on Pendle Hill in 1652 where he had a vision of 'a great people to be gathered'.

Shortly afterwards he came to Briggflatts, near Sedbergh, where he stayed the night with Richard Robinson and in 1675, when nonconformist meetings were still illegal, a Meeting House was built there, the oldest in the North and often considered the most beautiful in all England.

Originally with an earth floor and no ceiling but with holes in the roof which had to be plugged with moss, it was soon to be fitted with a ceiling, a wooden gallery and panelled walls, and at the foot of the stairs is a dog pen for sheepdogs accompanying their masters to the Meeting House.

It is worth seeing for its woodwork alone, but the simplicity and atmosphere of peace created by the silent worship of generations of Quakers make it a place that has to be experienced.

Site: about a mile (1.5km) south west of Sedbergh, just off the A683.
Grid Ref: SD 641912

The Summit of Disasters

Building the Settle–Carlisle Railway was an extraordinary feat requiring heroic effort in appalling conditions from the workforce and exceptional faith by those investing their capital.

Operating the railway was no less extraordinary. Gradients were steep, 1 in 100 being the ruling gradient for the whole of the 'Long Drag' of twenty-two miles (35km) from Settle to the summit of the line at Aisgill, and even steeper gradients on short stretches in the reverse direction from Carlisle. Weather conditions, too, were often horrendous. In 1946 the line was blocked by snow for two whole months and not infrequently trains were stranded for long periods, even lost entirely.

Not surprisingly there were accidents and two of the worst were near the summit of Aisgill.

In the early morning of Christmas Eve 1910 a signalman allowed a double-headed express to catch up and crash into two light engines, an error which led to a terrible fire. Then in September 1913 a southbound sleeper short of steam came to a standstill just north of the summit. Another night train also in difficulties because of poor coal overran signals and crashed into the sleeper. Once again fire broke out and fourteen people died.

Drivers and firemen must have sighed with relief when they passed the 1,169 feet (356m) summit sign.

Site: two miles (3km) north of the A684 on the B6259 just before Aisgill Moor cottages. Grid Ref: SD 779963

King Arthur and Lady Anne

In October 1663, at the age of seventy-four, Lady Anne Clifford set out from Skipton Castle to visit her other possessions, properties for which she had long fought to establish her rights. *En route* she stayed at Kilnsey and Nappa. Carried on a litter slung between two horses, it was a difficult journey, up Buckden Raikes, over the Stake Pass and into the wilds of Mallerstang, but eventually she arrived at her castle of Pendragon where she was to spend Christmas.

On an artificial hill, Pendragon was reputedly built by Uther Pendragon, father of King Arthur. Having been destroyed by the Scots in the sixteenth century, it was ruinous for over 100 years before Lady Anne restored it. Now ruinous again, it stands at the furthermost limits of the Yorkshire Dales, a gaunt reminder of the indomitable Lady Anne and her legendary predecessor.

Site: on the B6259 about four miles (6.5km) south of Kirkby Stephen.
Grid Ref: NY 782026

A Geologist's Granite Memorial

In 1815 Adam Sedgwick announced the victory at Trafalgar from a mounting block on the north side of the main street in Dent. Many years later a granite fountain was erected nearby in his honour.

Sedgwick, son of the local vicar, was born in 1785 and educated at Sedbergh and Cambridge, where he became professor of geology, a chair which he occupied for over fifty years. During that time he became internationally famous as a pioneer in his science. In 1985, to commemorate the 200th anniversary of Sedgwick's birth, a geology trail named after him was created. It runs along the River Clough to the east of Sedbergh.

Locally Sedgwick will also be remembered for a picture of Dent during his youth, which he wrote as part of a pamphlet (or 'memorial') aimed at restoring the status and the name of Cowgill Chapel, whose foundation stone he had laid. Thinking the name 'Cowgill' too vulgar, a curate had renamed the chapel 'Kirkthwaite'. Sedgwick was incensed and despatched his memorial to Prime Minister Gladstone and to the Queen. He had once been secretary to Prince Albert and had met the Queen. She intervened, an Act of Parliament was passed and Sedgwick got what he wanted.

Site: the fountain is in the centre of Dent, six miles (9.5km) south-west of Sedbergh; Cowgill Chapel is about three miles (5km) west of Dent).

Grid Ref: SD 705870

Gearstones

A very ordinary looking building on the roadside between Ribblehead and Hawes evokes memories of the great days of the eighteenth and early nineteenth centuries when drovers brought thousands of cattle from Scotland to the markets of England. The scale was immense. It is claimed that as many as 100,000 cattle were on the move at the same time and that a single man, a Mr Birtwhistle of Skipton, had 10,000, of which 5,000 might be seen together in Great Close, Malham.

The drovers were highly trusted, responsible men. Much wealth was in their care as they moved down through England at only a few miles per day. They had recognised stopping places and the Gearstones Inn was one of them. In 1792 Lord Torrington described it as 'filled with company ... the ground in front crowded by Scotch cattle and the drovers; and the house cramm'd by the buyers and sellers ...'

A scene hard to imagine today.

Site: on the B6255 about a mile (1.5km) north of the junction with B6479.
Grid Ref: SD 779799

Richmond and Swaledale

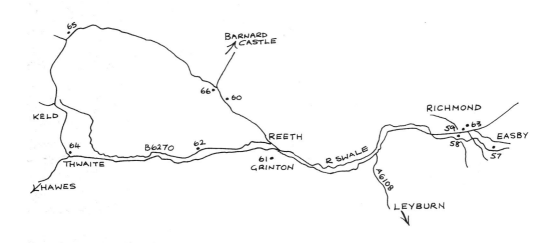

57. wall paintings, Easby Church
58. Culloden Tower, Richmond
59. Holy Trinity Church, Richmond
60. Langthwaite Bridge
61. lepers' squint, Grinton Church
62. Punch Bowl Inn, Low Row
63. Georgian Theatre, Richmond
64. Richard & Cherry Kearton
65. Tan Hill Inn
66. powder house, Langthwaite

Paintings on the Wall

Wall paintings were common in mediaeval churches. They were visual aids, the easiest way of teaching Bible stories and Christian belief to the illiterate. At St Agatha's, Easby, some fine paintings of the thirteenth century survive, the only extensive examples in the Dales. They are typical of their time, paintings of the fall of man in the Garden of Eden, of the birth and death of Christ, and domestic scenes of the four seasons, with figures in contemporary dress.

The church itself, undoubtedly an early one, was there before the adjacent abbey and may well have been a minster with priests having pastoral responsibilities. Its other major treasure is — or was, because the original is now in the Victoria and Albert Museum — a very early Northumbrian cross (right) dating from about the year 800. Parts were found embedded in the walls of the church and the top of the shaft was discovered in a field wall. A replica now stands in the church.

However, it is the wall paintings which are the most evocative, giving a tiny inkling of what it felt like to worship in a mediaeval church.

Site: from the B6271 out of Richmond, bear right on an unclassified road then right again in about three-quarters of a mile (1km) on a very minor road.

Grid Ref: NZ 185003

Culloden Tower

In 1746 Bonnie Prince Charlie made a last desperate attempt to achieve his objectives at Culloden. Facing much superior forces led by the Duke of Cumberland, he was defeated and his cause lost forever.

In Richmond the event was marked by the erection of the Culloden Tower on the site, indeed on the base, of an old castle (Hudswell Peele). Built by John Yorke, the local MP, and Anne, his wife, in what was later called the 'Gothick' style, it is a major landmark of the town. Its recently restored interior has magnificent chimney pieces and elaborate ceilings and, according to Pevsner, the building 'ought to be far better known'. Unfortunately it is not open to the public unless you are lucky enough to rent it from the Landmark Trust which uses it as a holiday cottage.

The tower is best seen from the Green, which was once an unsavoury part of Richmond but very different now.

Site: the Green is south-west of Richmond Castle down Cornforth Hill.
Grid Ref: NZ 169006

'The queerest ecclesiastical building one can imagine'

So said Nikolaus Pevsner speaking architecturally. But the history of Holy Trinity, Richmond, is equally queer. Built about 1150 as the parish church, it was soon too small and lost its status when St Mary's was built outside the town walls.

Having become ruinous it was rebuilt twice, first in 1360 and again in the sixteenth century. Under Queen Elizabeth's reign, part of the church — the north aisle — was used as a town hall and court, but in 1745 it became a church again, and then in the late nineteenth century a chapel for Richmond Grammar School.

At various times it has been a school, a warehouse, a refuge from the plague, had shops built under the north aisle, other shops inserted between the tower and nave, and the south aisle converted into cottages.

It is now the Museum of the Green Howards Regiment, but still contains a small chapel at the east end.

Site: in Richmond market square.

Grid Ref: NZ 171009

Herriot Country

The TV series of *All Creatures Great and Small* must have been one of the most popular series ever. Its success was partly a matter of the characters, partly the stories which were so very human and at the same time so intimately concerned with animals, and partly the scenery — wild moorland, beautiful valleys, ancient tracks and old farmhouses. Viewers were able to share a little in what James Herriot described as a wonderland which kept him permanently spellbound.

If you know the area well you might be able to identify the glimpses of countryside shown in each episode, but even if you are a stranger to the Dales you will know the scenes shown in the opening sequence. One is the ford on the road from Feetham to Arken-

garthdale, in the middle of leadmining country, and the other (pictured) is the bridge over Arkle Beck in the old mining village of Langthwaite.

Site: about three miles (4.5km) north-west of Reeth on the Arkengarthdale road.
Grid Ref: NZ 005025

The Lepers' Squint

A squint is an opening cut through a wall in a church to allow worshippers otherwise unsighted to watch the celebration of mass.

Such a hole cut through an external wall, sometimes called a 'low side window' or 'hagioscope', allowing people outside the church to witness proceedings at the altar within, are also often called 'lepers' squints' because it is assumed that lepers might have used them.

In fact lepers would not have been allowed anywhere near the church, and the real reason for these windows is not known, though it seems likely that they enabled someone outside the church to watch the mass and ring a bell to inform villagers not present of its progress.

A good example of a 'lepers' squint' is in the south wall of Grinton Church, at the south-west corner of the Blackburn chapel. While you are there, have a good look at the house next door — Blackburn House, pictured on the right — a fine example of vernacular architecture.

Site: a mile (1.5km) south-east of Reeth on the B6270.
Grid Ref: SE 046984

A Stop at the Punch Bowl

The corpse way in Swaledale is a very old route leading from Keld to Grinton Church, along which bodies from the upper dale were taken for burial. After 1580 a new burial ground at Muker removed the need for such a long journey, but before then it was a major task. Bodies wrapped in shrouds and placed in wicker baskets were carried by the men of the family, helped by regular pall-bearers from the villages on the way. From time to time there were stone slabs on which to rest their loads, but for those making the two-day journey a much longer rest was needed.

Leaving the body in the 'dead' house, a building close to Feetham, they would repair to the inn at Low Row, now called the Punch Bowl, for rest and refreshment. No doubt it was the arrival of two such parties which led to rather too much refreshment, and the placing of bodies in the wrong graves at Grinton!

Site: three miles (5km) west of Reeth on the B6270.
Grid Ref: SD 987985

Playground for the Rich at Richmond

An uninteresting look-ing building at Rich-mond houses one of the treasures of York-shire, indeed of Eng-land — the Georgian Theatre, the second oldest working theatre in the country.

Founded in 1788 by actor-manager Samuel Butler, who led his company round a group of theatres in the north of England, its two-month Rich-mond season at the time of the races was a tremendous success. But Butler's death in 1812 was followed by decline until, in 1848, its use as a theatre ceased and the build-ing was subsequently used for a variety of commercial purposes.

Fortunately, the internal fittings and decoration remain much as they were 200 years ago. Now refurbished, it is easy to enter another age as you tour the theatre and visit its museum. Still better is to go to a live performance because the theatre is now well used again.

Happily its prices are not as they were. From 1s to 3s, the present-day equivalent would be up to £100!

Site: a hundred yards (90m) north of Richmond market place.
Grid Ref: NZ 172010

Pioneers from Thwaite

Richard Kearton was born in Thwaite in 1862 and his brother Cherry in 1871. Lamed in his youth, Richard developed a keen interest in ornithology and by chance this led to work for Cassells publishers in London, where Cherry later joined him.

It was, however, natural history that fired them and was to become a full-time occupation. A box camera led to a book on birds' nests, and a bestseller *With Nature and a Camera* quickly followed.

Richard was soon a much sought-after lecturer and prolific author, while Cherry became a pioneer of natural history photography, the quality of his pictures being remarkable even by present-day standards. In due course his passion turned to movies. He toured the length and breadth of Africa and much of the rest of the world to film almost every conceivable creature.

The present popularity of natural history has its roots in the work of the Kearton brothers. Their own roots at Thwaite, the cottage in which they were born, is now marked with a delightful frieze of birds and animals carved in the lintel above the front door.

Site: approximately ten miles (16km) west of Reeth on the B6270. The cottage is in a row to your right as you enter Thwaite from the south.

Grid Ref: SD 893982

The Highest Public House in Britain

At 1,732 feet (528m), the Tan Hill Inn can be a very lonely spot, especially in winter.

Since it was built in 1737, when it was known as the Kings Pit after one of the local coalmines, it has been cut off by snow from the outside world almost every year. The worst was probably the winter of 1962-3 when the pub was cut off for thirteen weeks, and not only the lemonade froze but most of the spirits as well.

But it was always a welcoming place, with a fire constantly burning, for the miners who worked the nearby coalmines, for the drovers and other travellers passing by, and for farmers attending the sheep sales — perhaps the most important sales of Swaledale sheep anywhere.

Even so, the world in general knew little of Tan Hill until Mrs Susan Peacock, a former landlady, now commemorated by an inscribed slab of rock behind the pub, achieved fame through radio broadcasts in the 1930s. Since then it has been increasingly visited by tourists and, now the pub is almost astride the Pennine Way, walkers invariably call to sample the beer and the food.

The pub is now licensed for weddings, a good excuse for a visit if you really need one.

Site: four or five miles (6.5-8km) north of Keld.

Grid Ref: NY 897067

The Powder House

The hexagonal powder house at Langthwaite is probably the best preserved of all the buildings of the old Dales leadmines. Built early in the eighteenth century, it was owned by the CB Company, which had its origins in the purchase by a Dr Bathurst, physician to Oliver Cromwell, of all the mines in Arkengarthdale. His family developed the mines, some of the most profitable and long-lasting in the Dales, and Charles Bathurst, lord of the manor in the eighteenth century, had both the mines and a famous hotel named after him.

Powder houses, built for the storage of 'black powder' (gunpowder) before the days of dynamite, were strongly built and solitary. It was essential to keep the powder dry and safe from theft, and to minimise the potential damage of an explosion.

Site: Almost four miles (6.5km) north-west of Reeth near the junction of the Barnard Castle road with the Arkengarthdale road.

Grid Ref: NY 998034

Lower Wensleydale

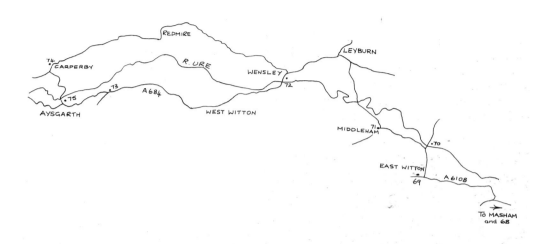

68. Druid's Temple
69. East Witton village
70. Ulshaw Bridge
71. Middleham Castle

72. reliquary, Wensley Church
73. follies, Swinithwaite
74. carved face, Carperby
75. rood screen, Aysgarth Church

Squire Danby's Stonehenge

A few miles from Masham near the village of Ilton stands a most bizarre collection of massive stones. Monoliths and trilithons (as at Stonehenge) stand in rough circles, while other stones form tomb-like structures or huge tables giving the appearance of sacrificial altars. It is no surprise that the place has long been called the 'Druid's Temple'.

It was in fact erected about 1820 by William Danby of Swinton Hall, who lived from 1752 to 1832. He intended it to be an attraction at a time when interest in druids was widespread. No doubt he hoped that it would be convincing, though his main purpopse was phil-anthropic, providing work and pay of one shilling per day for the unemployed. The labour involved is not known, but some of the stones weigh several tons, and moving them, setting them upright and indeed lifting them to form the cross pieces of the trilithons was a massive task.

Squire Danby is said to have posed a task of a quite different nature when he sought a man to live in the 'Temple' as a hermit for seven years in return for an annuity. The story that one 'hermit' lasted for four and a half years before abandoning his post is probably fictitious.

Site: a mile (1.5km) north of Ilton, which is three miles (5km) south-west of Masham, turn left down Knowles Lane.

Grid Ref: SE 174787

A Village Born Again

At the foot of Witton Fell lies the peaceful village of East Witton with its huge village green, the most extensive in the Dales and sometimes said to be the longest in England.

East Witton was a place of some importance in mediaeval times, probably owing its existence to the monks of Jervaulx, who seem to have established it on a brand-new site, and who had a corn mill and fulling mill there. But devastation by the plague caused the market to be moved to Ulshaw Bridge in 1563 and East Witton lost its importance.

In 1809 the Earl of Ailesby rebuilt the church and vicarage to mark the golden jubilee of George III. More or less simultaneously he rebuilt the village in stone, leaving it with the superb open space that exists today.

The village water tap at the bottom of the green is a late addition. It is attached to a boulder weighing three tons dragged there by a team of sixteen horses in 1859.

Site: two miles (3km) south-east of Middleham on the A6108.
Grid Ref: SE 144860

Bridges Galore

The Dales is a land of bridges. Some of the more primitive are in remote places, but clapper bridges can still be seen in, for example, Malham (left) and Linton, and packhorse bridges are legion. Except for those in very remote places, they have all been altered by widening or having their parapets raised. Good examples are at Linton, Wath and Ivelet, the latter having what some regard as the most graceful bridge of all. The bigger bridges such as the very handsome one at Hampsthwaite date mainly from the seventeenth century, and many on the Wharfe replace earlier bridges destroyed in a flood of 1673. Some like that at Kilgram may be earlier.

With so many to choose from, the one I pick as the most curious is the bridge at Ulshaw. It has a sundial of 1674 in one of its embrasures. A rare and delightful adornment.

Site: about a mile (1.5km) east of Middleham on a minor road leaving the A6108.

Grid Ref: SE 145872

The Windsor of the North

The first motte and bailey castle at Middleham, a little to the south-west of the existing castle, was on a much superior site, but the second castle, first built in the 1170s and extended later, became a place of kings, a place where Warwick the Kingmaker imprisoned Edward IV and from which Richard III left to be crowned king.

It is now a town devoted to the breeding and training of racehorses. They and their jockeys and grooms are everywhere, no doubt thankful that nowadays they no longer walk their horses to Newmarket as they once did.

But reminders of royalty remain. In one of the two market squares stands the swine cross (inset), said to represent the boar of Richard III, and in the church is a replica of the Middleham jewel, found in 1985 near the castle once known as the Windsor of the North.

Site: Middleham is on the A6108 leading south from Leyburn.

Grid Ref (Swine Cross): SE 126877

Riches at Wensley

Wensley was a market town from 1306 and was by far the most important settlement in the dale. Sadly a plague of 1563 was so disastrous that those who did not die fled. Wensley was deserted and never recovered its status.

What remains is one of the finest churches in the Dales in what seems to be a sleepy little hamlet in a most un-Daleslike setting. To describe its riches would take too long. It has a family pew of the Scropes from Castle Bolton constructed with parts of a screen from Easby Abbey, poppy-head furnishings from the Ripon school of carvers, and an eighteenth century two-decker pulpit. It has a fourteenth century brass to Sir Simon de Wenslaw, one of the finest brasses in England, and what may be a wooden reliquary which at one time would have contained relics of a saint, also transported from Easby Abbey.

If you want more, look in the churchyard for a memorial to the surgeon who served with Nelson at Trafalgar and was with him at his death, and another to the comedian Al Read.

Site: two miles (3km) south-west of Leyburn on the A684.
Grid Ref: SE 092895

Oddities at Swinithwaite

On the roadside at Swinithwaite is a stone inscribed with the cross of the Knights Templar, a body of knights formed to protect pilgrims on their way to Jerusalem. It is a reminder that they had an establishment nearby at Penhill. Unfortunately the conduct of the Templars was far from exemplary, the organisation was dissolved in 1312 and now, despite a

period of ownership by the Knights Hospitallers, nothing remains to be seen apart from the foundations of a chapel and some stone tombs, and even these only by those capable of a little hard walking. But the roadside stone can be seen and next to it a modern rarity, a marker indicating the boundary between Aysgarth and Leyburn rural district councils.

Rare or interesting as these might be, they are insignificant compared to the curiosities to be found only a few hundred yards away to the left of the road to West Burton. Per-

haps the strangest of all Dales follies, astonishingly quite modern, are a 'pepper pot' of 1921 (left) and a 'space ship' (right) built about 1860. Like some older follies, it seems that they were built to give work to the unemployed but also no doubt to enhance the view from the house below.

Site: On the A684, two miles (3km) east of Aysgarth close to the Slapestone Wath footpath.

Grid Ref: SE 028889

The Face of Carperby

Stone faces, often crudely carved, are found in many places — on the gable end of a barn in Thorpe, in St Helen's Well at Eshton, on the arches of the church at Kirkby Malham and so on. Clearly they are not purely decorative, though their purpose is not easy to see.

Their origin is probably pagan. In the Celtic world the human head was regarded as symbolic of powerful forces for good, good luck, good health and protection against the forces of evil, and the deliberate assimilation of pagan practice by the early Christian church made it inevitable that curious faces gaze at us from curious places such as those at Kirkby Malham.

Even so, I still find it extremely odd that a face should have been carved in the end of one of the arms of the 1674 village cross at Carperby.

Site: Carperby is about a mile (1.5km) north of Aysgarth on a minor road.
Grid Ref: SE 007897

The Jervaulx Treasures

Until the middle of the sixteenth century, every parish church in England would have had a rood screen separating nave from chancel and supporting a crucifix flanked by Mary and St John. The screen in Aysgarth Church, now on the south side of the chancel, is probably the most magnificent piece of mediaeval wood carving in the Dales. Restored and richly painted, it has a quite extraordinary impact.

Nearby, the vicar's stall has a rebus (a pictorial riddle) of a hazel tree and a 'ton' or barrel commemorating William de Heslington, Abbot of Jervaulx in 1472. That and other evidence suggests that these treasures came from Jervaulx at the time of the Dissolution of the Monasteries, and legend has it that the screen was carried shoulder-high by twenty men.

But there is no certainty. It may have been given to Aysgarth by Jervaulx and be the work of a renowned school of wood carvers at Ripon but, whatever the truth, the screen is worth going a long way to see.

Incidentally, the churchyard is the largest in the country.

Site: the church is on a minor road leading north from the A684.
Grid Ref: SE 012885

Upper Wensleydale

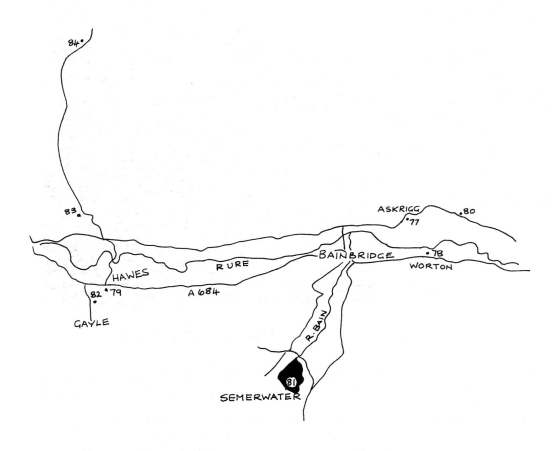

77. market cross, Askrigg
78. wall tablet, Worton
79. Kit Calvert
80. Nappa Hall

81. Semerwater
82. Gayle Mill
83. Hardraw Force
84. the Buttertubs

Bulls and Bears

The original 'Skeldale House' of the TV series *All Creatures Great and Small* is in Askrigg, and for that reason the town has become a tourist attraction. It is well worth visiting for other reasons.

Its impressive church has a very fine nave ceiling and, outside, a monument to 'an honest attorney', believed to be the only one in the country!

Standing with one's back to the church, 'Skeldale House' is on the right, and immediately in front is the market cross. It is said that a bear pit was nearby. True or not, it was certainly the place for bull-baiting: the ring to which the bulls were tethered remains embedded in a stone.

For a time it was a legal requirement that bulls were baited before being slaughtered and sold for meat. Happily for Mr Herriot and his colleagues, the practice was outlawed in 1835.

Site: Askrigg is reached by a minor road from the A684 about two miles (3km) northeast of Bainbridge.

Grid Ref: SD 948910

Writings on the Wall

On a hotel in Hawes, once a Quaker building, there is inscribed 'Ano Dom 1668. God being with us who can be against', and in West Witton there are several similar godfearing inscriptions. At Carlton in Coverdale is a somewhat more self-centred tablet erected by Henry Constantine in 1861, in which he describes himself as 'The Coverdale Bard' and writes verse which begins:

'He wrote from knowledge, genius kind'

An epitaph in his own lifetime!

Rather more agreeable is the modest tablet at Worton erected by Michael Smith and dated 1729, in which he proudly declares himself the 'mechanick' of his house. He wanted the world to know that he built it himself, but at the same time he acknowledged that his maker was his better when he added 'But He that built all things is God'.

Site: two miles (3km) east of Bainbridge on the A684.

Grid Ref: SD 955900

'One man in his time ...'

Kit Calvert, born in 1903 at Burtersett, the son of a quarryman, started work at twelve as a labourer for five shillings a week. He was destined to be one of the most loved and respected men ever to come from Hawes, and left behind him legacies for which he will be long remembered.

In 1933 he rescued the insolvent Hawes Dairy and provided scores of jobs both there and throughout Wensleydale. (The photograph shows the old Wensleydale Dairy to the right of Gayle Beck.) He established a bookshop which was and remains

a delight for all booklovers to visit. He was a fount of knowledge on all matters concerning Wensleydale, and translated parts of the Bible into its dialect. He engaged in battle with the authorities to provide a playground for children in Hawes — and won.

Eventually in 1977 he was awarded an MBE at Buckingham Palace. I like to think that he was still smoking his churchwarden's clay pipe.

Site: the old creamery is in the middle of Hawes just upstream from the bridge.
Grid Ref: SD 874898

Nappa

Nappa Hall in Wensleydale, dating from 1459, is the only remaining house of the pele (fortified tower) type in the Dales. Another rather earlier example at Hellifield is ruinous. Although by no means secure against a determined attack, such houses would provide a fair measure of protection against small groups of marauding robbers.

That at Nappa was built by Thomas Metcalfe who had fought at Agincourt and whose family still live there. It has two towers. The smaller, of two stories, contained service rooms and probably once housed a chapel, while the larger, of four stories, contained the main living accommodation. Between them is a hall which had a minstrel gallery.

In 1556, one of the family, Sir Christopher, who was High Sheriff, attended the assizes at York with no less than 300 of his Metcalfe kinsmen, all riding white horses. (The family is still said to be the largest in the Dales.) He later entertained Mary Queen of Scots, whose ghost used to haunt the hall until her bed was removed in the last century.

Site: Nappa is a little over a mile (1.5km) east of Askrigg on a minor road.

Grid Ref: SD 965908

Legends of the Lake

'Semerwater rise, Semerwater sink, and cover all save this li'le house that gave me meat and drink.'

So cried an angel, disguised as an old man, who had begged for food. Only a very poor family had given him food and shelter, and his cry immediately caused such enormous floods that every house vanished except that of the old man and his wife.

That is the legend. The fact is that Iron Age lake dwellings have been found here.

Another legend relates that the huge limestone boulder at the north end of the lake — the Carlow Stone — was dropped by a giant when throwing it at the Devil, but the plain fact is that it was brought by a glacier.

A place of legend. Also a place of beauty which can be serene or tempestuous, but always worth seeing.

Incidentally, the River Bain which flows out of the lake is only 2½ miles (4km) long, the shortest river in Britain.

Site: Semerwater is just over two miles (3km) south-west of Bainbridge.

Grid Ref: SD 922875 (of Carlow Stone and parking)

A Record-Breaking Mill

The mill at Gayle is one of the oldest surviving mills of the Dales, dating from the 1780s when people for whom spinning and weaving had been cotttage industries were beginning to work in factories. At first it was a cottton mill, then a flax mill and, later, wool. Then in the mid-nineteenth century is was converted to be used as a saw mill and joiner's shop. Its twenty foot (6m) water wheel was superseded by a water turbine in 1879, and a second turbine was installed in the 1920s by the Hawes Electric Lighting Company to provide electricity for the inhabitants of Gayle and Hawes.

Water from a dam 350 yards (320m) upstream was released into the beck by a sluice, and then diverted by a weir underneath Gayle Bridge into a still existing stone and wood leat (pictured) and then to the water wheel.

Specially long timbers from America were imported for construction of the mill, each floor of which has an open working space with a twenty-eight foot (8.5m) span, and particularly for the pitch pine king-post roof in the attic. But what the mill is most famous for is its turbine, the oldest working turbine in Europe and probably the world.

Site: the mill is about half a mile (0.8km) from Hawes, a short way downstream from the bridge in Gayle village.

Grid Ref: SD 872894

A Force to be Reckoned with

At almost 100 feet (30m), Hardraw Force is the highest unbroken waterfall in England. After visits by Wordsworth and Turner it became a place of popular pilgrimage in the late eighteenth century and then, in 1885, a venue for a band contest, revived in recent years. Special trains brought crowds to hear some of the best bands in England. Once, early this century, the crowds had an extra treat. Blondin, the tight-rope walker, was there to cross the ravine; for good measure he cooked an omelette in the middle.

You approach the force through the Green Dragon Inn, paying a small fee. If you are sure-footed or foolhardy you can even walk behind the falls: an extraordinary experience, particularly if there has been heavy rain. You might even look for fossils. Footprints in a piece of flagstone found by schoolchildren a few years ago turned out to be those of an armoured, flesh-eating amphibian, the oldest tracks of a four-legged animal yet found in Britain.

Floods have destroyed the lip of the falls on several occasions, most recently in 1890 when Lord Wharncliffe, the owner, had it restored to its original condition. Hardraw Force has frozen twice. In 1740 it became 'a cone of ice 90ft in height and as much in circumference at its base', and in 1881 'the cascade congealed and the water was observed to flow through a glass tube'.

A cooling thought as you sit in the September sun listening to the bands!

Site: the Green Dragon is a little over a mile (1.5km) north-west of Hawes.
Grid Ref: NY 867913

The Buttertubs

The road from Hawes to Thwaite is one of those grand, high moorland routes with views that seem as if you can see for ever. Alongside the road are the Buttertubs, curious geological features fantastically shaped by rainwater which are so deep that you cannot see the bottom.

Asked how deep they were, a farmer is said to have replied: 'That one's bottomless … but over there is one that's even deeper!'

They are in fact up to eighty feet (24m) deep, and it is wise not to get too close to peer down into them: it can cause vertigo even in those not usually affected.

How they got their name is not clear, but it is commonly assumed that there is some similarity of shape to the kind of tubs actually used by farmers. You need a good imagination to accept that. I prefer the theory that farmers on the way back from Hawes market would lower their unsold butter down by rope and leave it there until next market day.

Site: about two miles (3km) south of Thwaite.
Grid Ref: SD 874961

Nidderdale

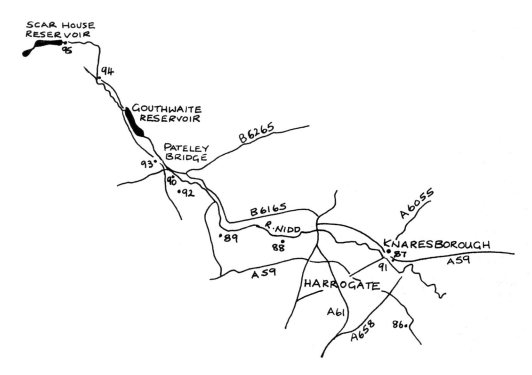

86. ‘Blind Jack’ Metcalfe
87. Oldest Chemist’s Shop, Knaresborough
88. tomb, Hampsthwaite Church
89. thatched house, Holme
90. chapel, Bewerley

91. Chapel of Our Lady of the Crag, Knaresborough
92. Two Stoops
93. water wheel, Pateley Bridge
94. drinking fountain, Lofthouse
95. Scar House village

A Man of Vision

John Metcalfe was born at Knaresborough in 1717. Though blinded by smallpox at six, he had an active childhood and eventually, after an elopement, married a girl described as the prettiest in Harrogate.

He was a man of many parts: hirer of carriages, fish merchant, timber merchant, guide and smuggler. He also played the fiddle for the British Army which fought at Culloden, and for parties and dances around Harrogate. But above all he made roads and built bridges.

Contracts came his way from Yorkshire, Lancashire and Derbyshire, and in all he built almost 200 miles (320km) of roads with a peak workforce of several hundred men. He not only organised and managed this major enterprise but also stumped the country surveying routes. One was over the Pennines to Huddersfield across land previously regarded as impassable. His work was of such a standard that he has been called the first of the great road engineers.

John, forever to be remembered as 'Blind Jack', died in 1810 and was buried at Spofforth. A truly amazing man.

Site: Spofforth is about five miles (8km) south-west of Harrogate on the A661.
Grid Ref: NY 365511

Buy my Sweet Lavender

Knaresborough market, which was a corn market of great importance in the eighteenth century, dates from 1310 and some of the buildings in the market place may well have their origins in that century. The external appearances are of course of a much later date, but even so are still of a considerable age.

One of them declares itself to be the oldest chemist's shop in England, and the claim may indeed be absolutely true because there is said to be proof that the premises have been in continuous use an an apothecary's and pharmacy since 1720.

The eighteenth century box windows with what are described as Chinese Chippendale legs are extremely attractive, and so is the atmosphere within. While you are there, do try some of the shop's own lavender water made from an ancient secret recipe.

Site: the market place is just off the A59 in the centre of the town.
Grid Ref: SE 351571

The Most Beautiful Tomb in Yorkshire?

Amy Woodforde-Finden was born in Valparaiso in 1860 where her father was British Consul. Later, after her marriage, she lived for a while in India. On her return to England she wrote *Indian Love Lyrics*. She died in 1919 and is buried in the church of St Thomas à Becket at Hampsthwaite. Her tomb is of marble — a brilliant shining white — on it are carved scenes and flowers reminding us of her lyrics. To some it looks too sugary, oversweet and sentimental, but to others — me included — it has a rare pristine beauty.

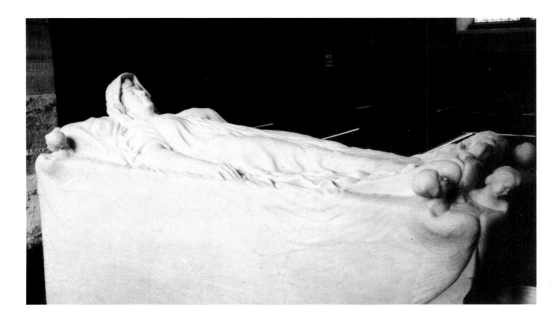

The dedication of the church to St Thomas à Becket is very rare. It was reputedly built by four knights who had murdered St Thomas in his cathedral at Canterbury in 1170. One of them was Hugh de Morville, Lord of Knaresborough, and after the murder the four took refuge in Knaresborough Castle. Eventually they were forced to surrender, and the task of building the church in honour of their victim was imposed as a penance.

Incidentally, the porch of Hampsthwaite Church is remarkable for the large number of ancient stone coffin-lids incorporated in the structure.

Site: Leave the A59 northwards about three miles (5km) west of Harrogate.

Grid Ref: SE 259591

A Unique Holme

Thatched roofs, mainly of ling, were once very common in the Dales.

They seem to have been especially common in Swaledale where quite a number of small miners' cottages remained thatched until the middle of the last century. For small barns and cowhouses, thatching remained in use until the beginning of the present century.

Gradually thatch disappeared, the immediate cause of its disappearance usually being the wish of the householder to raise the roof so as to allow two full stories. It was then easier to have a slate or stone roof with a much flatter pitch.

Only one thatched house remains, the Holme at Darley, which was encased in stone in 1667 when it was slightly extended so as to provide an external chimney. Though a private residence, it can be seen clearly from the roadside.

There was no pressing need to raise the roof of barns, and there are still a few with vestiges of thatch. There is also a reconstructed thatched barn on the edge of Grimwith Reservoir.

Site: approximately two miles (3km) east of the B6451, through Darley.
Grid Ref: SE 217597

From Monastic Chapel to School and Back Again

In 1175, Roger de Mowbray, in return for finance for a journey to Jerusalem, gave lands at Bewerley, including a chapel, to Fountains Abbey. The monks established a grange there, which remained in their possession until the Dissolution of the Monasteries.

Marmaduke Huby, who was abbot from 1494 to 1526, had the present chapel built and his initials can be seen on the exterior walls, as well as an inscription (left) which, translated, reads 'To God Alone Honour and Glory', Huby's own motto which also appears on his great tower at Fountains.

The land and buildings changed hands on several occasions, and in 1678 it became a school and schoolhouse. So it remained continuously until 1818 and for substantial periods of time thereafter, still with a dwelling house under the same roof as the west end.

In the 1960s it was restored and rededicated. As a small, simple chapel it seems a place set aside from the world.

Site: approximately 600 yards (550m) from the B6265, turning left for a short way from Pateley Bridge town centre.

Grid Ref: SE 158647

The Chapel of Our Lady of the Crag

About 1408, John the Mason cut out of the solid rock a wayside shrine on the way to the Priory of St Robert near Knaresborough. It is small, damp and gloomy, but still retains something of the atmosphere of a holy place. The door, window, altar and all the architectural features are in a very early primitive style.

It is a curious place and its curiosity is heightened immensely by a large figure in full armour on guard at the entrance. It was added in the sixteenth century and is often assumed to represent St Robert, a hermit who lived in a cave near Grimhall Bridge, performed miraculous cures and was benevolent to the needy. A more likely possibility is that it represents a Knight Templar because it is not far away from a former establishment of the Templars. Whoever he is, he appears to have had his face renewed, probably in the last century.

Site: about 200 yards (180m) along Abbey Road from Low Bridge, Knaresborough.
Grid Ref: SE 351565

The Folly of John Yorke

The Yorke family is one of the great families of Yorkshire. Bewerley Hall was their seat, but branches of the family stretched widely from Gowthwaite Hall (now under the waters of the reservoir) to York and Richmond. Their wealth enabled them to be philanthropic. Benefactions to the church at Pateley Bridge and gifts of land for a school at Greenhow were typical, and John Yorke (who died in 1813) was particularly concerned by the hardship of unemployment.

He had long wanted to erect a structure similar to one he had seen abroad and, late in the eighteenth century, he set unemployed men building what we now know as Yorke's Folly on Guisecliff overlooking Pateley Bridge. Originally there were three columns but one was blown down in a gale of 1893. The two that remain are impressive enough and are easily accessible. They are locally known as the Two Stoops.

The view from them is magnificent, from Whernside in the west to the Yorkshire Wolds in the east. On a clear day you will see York Minster.

Site: approximately 1½ miles (2.5km) south of Pateley Bridge; from the B6265 through Bewerley.

Grid Ref: SE 157635

A Thirty Horse-Power Water Wheel

The flax and hemp trade was a major industry of Nidderdale for a long time, and from the seventeenth century linen became more important than wool. It was, however, the development of machine spinning at the end of the eighteenth century which provided a crucial boost. Mills powered by water wheels soon became common.

One such mill was at Foster Beck near Pateley Bridge, built in 1864 for spinning heavy flax-yarn. It had a chequered history and finally closed in 1966. In its later years at any rate it had few employees, and it was the difficulty of obtaining labour together with damage to its water wheel which was the immediate cause of closure.

The wheel is still there. With a diameter

of thirty-four feet (10.5km) and five feet (1.5m) broad, it is one of the county's largest 'overshot' wheels, in which the water providing the power strikes at that part of the wheel beginning its downward path. It was in use until the mill closed, and was fully restored in 1990 as a feature in the grounds of the Watermill Inn.

Site: approximately a mile (1.5km) north-west of Pateley Bridge on the road to Lofthouse.

Grid Ref: SE 148664

A Fount of Good Advice

Troughs for animals and taps or fountains for people abound in the Dales; after all it is not long since few of us had our own taps.

In Burnsall, for example, there are three communal taps provided by Bradford Corporation when it began to take water from local becks and deprived villagers of their traditional supplies.

Some fountains are commemorative. The grandest of all is undoubtedly one at Bolton Abbey, paid for by public subscription after Lord Frederick Cavendish MP was assassinated in Dublin.

Much simpler is one at Lofthouse built in 1920 as a war memorial. It has this homespun advice:

'A Pint of Cold Water Three Times a Day is the Surest Way to Keep Doctor Away. Whoso Thirsteth Let Him Come Hither and Drink'
    and:

'If You Want to be Healthy, Wealthy and Stout,
Use Plenty of Cold Water Inside and Out'
    But why stout?

Site: approximately seven miles (11km) north-west of Pateley Bridge.
Grid Ref: SE 101735

A Lost Village

You have to use your imagination to see this curiosity.

A short way down the valley from the dam at Scar House Reservoir in Upper Nidderdale, there are a series of platforms which visitors find puzzling. They might well have been bases for huts in some kind of military establishment; but they are not.

They are in fact the remains of a former village which housed the men who built the dam. At first they lived in the old warehouse at Pateley Bridge — now a superb museum — but that was not big enough nor near enough to the construction site, so Scar village was built.

It housed no less than 700 workmen. There were shops, a cinema, a chapel, 30 bungalows, 28 houses and 16 hostels each for 62 single men. There was also a school for 100 children, a doctor, a village fire brigade and a railway station.

The dam, completed in 1936, rises no less than 150 feet (46m) and the wall is 600 yards (550m) across. It is said to be the largest masonry dam in Europe. The capacity of the reservoir is over two thousand million gallons (9,000 million litres).

The canteen at Scar village was given a new lease of life and became the village hall of Darley.

Site: the dam is about ten miles (16km) north-west of Pateley Bridge and can be reached by a toll road from the village of Lofthouse.

Grid Ref: NY 075767

In and Around Ripon

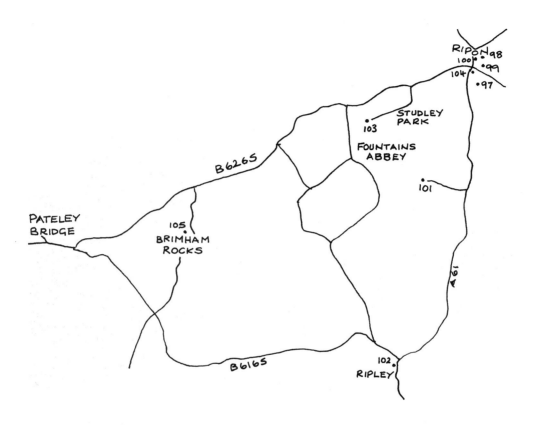

97. Navigation Inn, Ripon
98. Prison & Police Museum, Ripon
99. gravestone, Ripon Cathedral
100. lamppost, Ripon
101. Markenfield Hall

102. Ripley village
103. Studley Royal
104. Wakeman's House, Ripon
105. Brimham Rocks

By Boat to Ripon

What is a pub called the Navigation doing in a city like Ripon? The answer lies nearby — a canal whose existence few suspect.

Ripon has always been an important commercial centre, trading in textiles, leather and livestock, but by the time the city wished to export lead and dairy produce and import coal, there were problems.

The fear of losing trade to others led to an Act of Parliament for a navigable waterway linking the city with the River Ure. It was built by the engineer John Smeaton between 1767 and 1773, but it was not long before it was in financial trouble and by 1845 the railway had appeared. Now all that remains is a distinctly unnavigable stretch of water, some derelict warehouses and the Navigation to remind us of what might have been.

However, redevelopment to create a thriving new waterside is in prospect. Let us hope.

Site: Canal Road is off Bondgate Green which is across the river south of the cathedral.
Grid Ref: SE 318708

How About a Spell in the Cells?

In St Marygate, Ripon, stands a rather bleak-looking building which was erected in 1686 as a house of correction for vagabonds and beggars.

It was extended in the early nineteenth cenury to house other kinds of prisoner, and it continued in use as a prison until it was closed by the order of the home secretary in 1887. It remained in use as Ripon Police Station until 1956.

Its connection with the law is still retained, for it now houses the Prison and Police Museum, a superb specialist museum which concerns itself with the history of crime and punishment generally, not merely the story of law and order in Ripon since the days of the wakeman.

If you want to know what it feel like to be confined and have the iron bars of a cell closed behind you — and who doesn't — this is the place to visit.

The workhouse has also recently been restored, and it has been opened as a museum too.

Site: a short way along St Marygate which runs north from the cathedral.
Grid Ref: SE 315713

Gone Fishing

Tombstones with epitaphs are fascinating and collecting them can be an absorbing pastime.

Some declare piously that death had long been hoped for, while others, equally pious, describe the deceased with an almost endless string of impossibly laudatory adjectives. All too many record sad lives with many deaths of infant children, while others record eventful lives such as one at Wensley of a surgeon who served on the *Victory* at Trafalgar.

For the collector, those which suggest simple, uneventful, but successful lives are pleasing rarities. One such at Linton for brothers John and Henry Davis describes their outstanding singing voices. Even better are those which amuse. One, at Ripon, for Bryan Tunstall who died in 1790, reads: 'He was a most expert angler, until Death, envious of his Merit, threw out his line, hook'd him and landed him here.'

Site: in the graveyard close to the east end of Ripon Cathedral.

Grid Ref: SE 317712

A Relic Lamppost

It is surprising to walk down an ordinary street in Ripon and be suddenly confronted by a tall, elegant and beautifully maintained lamppost. There is nothing like it anywhere else in the city nor in any other place that I am aware of. Why?

It is in fact a relic of early Victorian times when methane gas from the city's sewers was harnessed to provide street lights for Ripon. Thanks to the local Civic Society it has been refurbished and, moreover, it works.

Site: in Victorian Grove which leads northwards out of the main car park.

Grid Ref: SE 314714

A Treasure Hard to Find

Markenfield Hall is one of my favourite places, partly because I first found it by accident, before I ever read about it, when walking from Fountains Abbey, but mainly because of what it is.

Built by Sir Thomas Markenfield in 1310 when he was granted a license to crenellate (fortify with battlements), it is an extraordinary

survival, a mediaeval moated manor-house with first floor hall, adjoining great chamber and chapel. Its gatehouse dates from later, Tudor times.

Markenfield has been called the finest moated house in England. It is open only on Mondays in summer and access is not at all easy, but do persevere and do not expect a furnished, lived-in house. A farmer lives in one wing and Baron Grantley has rooms in the hall, but what you see has been empty for a long time. That is fine because you see it as it was, little altered. Sheer delight.

Site: turn right from the A61 three miles (5km) south of Ripon on Hell Wath Lane.
Grid Ref: SE 295674

A Village from Alsace

Do visit Ripley. The castle is full of interest and so is the church with its unique weeping cross. But take a good look at the village itself. You will no doubt find it a little odd. None of the houses are old as they are in most villages hereabouts, and all are in a uniform style but not the local vernacular.

The old village was in fact completely destroyed in the early nineteenth century when Sir William Ancotts Ingilby completed the new village which he had begun in the 1780s. He was an eccentric, besotted with Alsace Lorraine in eastern France, and it was from there that he imported the style. And not only the style, the language as well. Above a small door in the fifteenth century gatehouse of the castle, those seeking entrance are enjoined to 'parlez au Suisse' (speak Swiss), and one of the largest buildings in the village, now the post office, proudly proclaims itself to be the 'Hotel de ville' or town hall.

Site: the village is just off the A61, about four miles (6.5km) north of Harrogate.
Grid Ref: SE 285606

Delights in a Deer Park

The original home of John Aislabie at Studley Royal was burned down in 1945, but the parkland which surrounded it remains a favourite place for walkers, picnickers and those who love watching the three herds of deer — fallow, red and sika.

There are also two architectural treasures. One is the original stable block (left), now a private house, built in 1716-1720 and a fine example of the architecture of

the period. The second is St Mary's Church (below), at the head of an enormously long avenue of trees which leads one's eyes to the distant Ripon Cathedral.

It was built in the 1870s by the Marchioness of Ripon as a memorial to Frederick Vyner, her son, killed by Greek bandits. Its style is Early English and the theme of the interior was 'Paradise Lost and Regained', but what is so remarkable about it is its

sheer opulence. Expense was no object, and it is said to have cost £50,000. Statues, windows, ironwork, wood carving, mosaics and the tombs of the marchioness and her husband are all of the highest quality; colours and materials are rich.

Site: about four miles (6.5km) west of Ripon off the B6265 to Pateley Bridge.

Grid Ref: SE 275693

'Except Ye Lord Keep Ye City Ye Wakeman Waketh In Vain'

That is the motto of Ripon.

The office of wakeman has ancient origins. Whoever held it had the job of keeping the peace in the city from 9pm in the evening, when the hornblower blows his horn in the market place, until dawn. He had constables patrolling the streets and no doubt was glad when they had a peaceful night and did not arouse him, not only because of losing his sleep but because he had to compensate those suffering burglary. However, he did have the right to levy a tax for this purpose — 4d for houses with two doors and 2d for those with one.

The last wakeman and first mayor of Ripon in 1604 was Hugh Ripley, and his house is now called the Wakeman's House. What can be seen today is really one wing of a much larger house, the rest having been demolished.

Even so, it splendidly complements the magnificent neighbouring town hall on which the city's motto is emblazoned.

Site: on the south side of Ripon market.

Grid Ref: SE 312712

A Natural Sculpture Park

Question: Where can you find an eagle, a turtle, an anvil, a dancing bear and a druid's writing desk?

Answer: At Brimham Rocks, not the only place with curiously shaped rocks but certainly Yorkshire's best, a result of millions of years of ice and wind.

Brimham was first developed as a grange by the monks of Fountains Abbey. Much later, in 1792, Lord Grantley built Brimham House, now a National Trust Information Centre, as a shooting lodge. By then the rocks had been 'discovered' by travellers seeking the picturesque and grotesque, and the area became popular with the Victorians as a playground and even as a place of religious assembly. In 1885 a Wesleyan rally attracted 3,000 people, the crowds enjoying a feast and a couple of sermons.

Today we go not for sermons but to enjoy the bizarre natural sculptures and the superb views over Nidderdale and the Plain of York to the east.

Site: turn south on a minor road from the B6265 about four miles (6.5km) east of Pateley Bridge.

Grid Ref: SE 208648

Otley and Washburndale

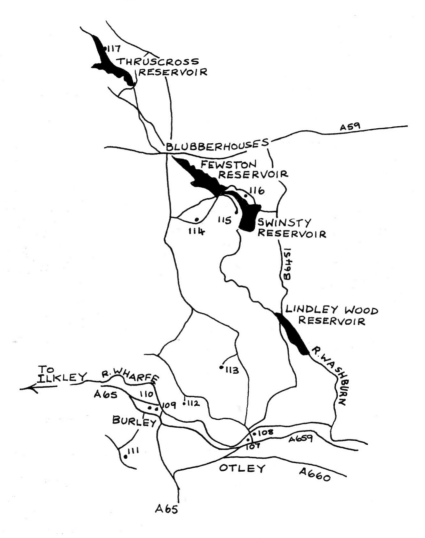

107. memorial, Otley Church
108. Thomas Chippendale
109. Iron Row, Burley
110. W E Forster
111. Job the Hermit
112. Weston Church

113. Clifton village
114. Robinson Library, Timble
115. Swinsty Hall
116. gravestones, Fewston Church
117. West End sunken village

A Unique Memorial

It is not often that a churchyard memorial becomes a Grade II listed building, but there is one in Otley.

It is a memorial to those who were killed during the construction of the nearby Bramhope railway tunnel. Over 2,000 men and 400 horses were involved in the work, a most difficult and hazardous enterprise bedevilled by severe floods. Deaths from drowning added to those from pneumonia and a wide variety of accidents, though the absence of records means that the total numbers are not known.

James Bray, the tunnel contractor, had the memorial built to twenty-three of the dead whose names are known. It is an exact replica of the entrance to the tunnel. From time to time it has been in a sad state of disrepair but, most recently, British Rail contributed £5,000 towards its maintenance and it is now in a state worthy of those it commemorates.

Site: 100 yards (90m) south of Otley Market Place alongside the parish church.
Grid Ref: SE 202454

From Otley
to a Fortune
in London

Probably Otley's most famous son, Thomas Chippendale was born in 1718, the son of a joiner. For some time he lived with an uncle in a cottage in Bondgate, which still exists and is now marked with a plaque.

Having completed an apprenticeship with his father, he left Otley in 1739 and from then on he worked in London, where he married and eventually died. Even so, some of his finest work can be seen locally, for example in Harewood House. It seems likely that the owners, the Lascelles family, knew of Chippendale's talents when he was a young man in Otley.

Soon he became famous throughout England, and now the quality of his work, particularly his chairs, is recognised worldwide.

For a long time his association with Otley was overlooked, but his statue now stands outside the old grammar school which he probably attended.

Site: fifty yards (45m) north of Otley market place.

Grid Ref: SE 202456

Burley's Iron Row

No one knows for sure why Iron Row is so called, though the most appealing theory is that an iron door or gate was erected as a defence against Luddite gangs.

Be that as it may, it was first called New Row when it was built in 1800 by Messrs Greenwood and Whitaker for the employees of their nearby mills.

In 1848 the row was on the market and the houses were then described as fireproof. They probably were. What were then one-up, one-down houses (they have since been extended) were built entirely without wood. The floor of the main room was stone and so was the staircase leading out of it to the room above. The floor of the upper room was also stone, supported by a barrel-vaulted roof in what was and still is the main room of the house. A unique construction? I do not know, but I suspect that it is.

Site: Iron Row runs out of Main Street, Burley, a short way to the east of the mini-roundabout.

Grid Ref: SE 167464

A Victorian Philanthropist

Born in 1818 of a Quaker family, William Edward Forster started a textile business in Bradford in partnership with William Fison. He and his wife, the daughter of Dr Arnold of Rugby, moved to Burley in 1852, the worsted manufacturing business having already moved there.

Successful in business and with a strong social conscience, Forster took a great interest in both local and national affairs. Locally he dedicated himself to the provision of better sanitary conditions and to education, especially for the 'half-timers' (children who worked one half of the day and went to school in the other) at his own mill.

From 1868 their school was in a building provided by Forster and Fison, which also housed a lecture hall, a reading room and a concert hall. Memorials to them both now stand in front of the building, now used as a village hall.

In 1861 Forster became MP for Bradford and, as the minister responsible, he introduced the Education Act of 1870, a truly great memorial.

Site: on Burley Main Street.

Grid Ref: SE 166464

Job the Hermit

Born illegitimate about 1780, Job Senior was given the name of his mother who brought him up in Ilkley. After earning his living by odd-jobbing on local farms, he suddenly came into money when his father, following an attack of conscience, left him a legacy. Job took to drink, spent his legacy and subsequently bought his ale by singing in pubs.

In an attempt to secure his future he married a cottage-owning widow much older than himself, but her death merely prompted her relatives to destroy the cottage so that he would not inherit. Job became a hermit living in Burley Woodhead among the ruins.

His ragged, disreputable appearance and lifestyle soon made him an attraction to tourists, and as weather forecaster and 'agony aunt' he became ever more popular, until he died of cholera in 1857.

If only he could have known that a nearby inn, the Woolpack, was soon to change its name to the Hermit.

Site: leave Burley centre on Station Road, turn left at T-junction to find the Hermit in approximately 300 yards (275m).

Grid Ref: SE 154448

Surprises at Weston

One of the most secluded churches of the area is at Weston. As you approach it down a very narrow dead-end road you pass the Elizabethan mansion of Weston Hall, for centuries the home of the Vavasours.

Behind it but invisible from the road is its late sixteenth century banquetting house, a pure gem. Only occasionally can the public see it, but if the chance arises, take it.

As might be expected, the church — which is basically Norman but which has undergone many changes since — has had long and close associations with the Vavasours, and has a 'squire's parlour' with fireplace to keep the family warm even though the rest of the congregation might be freezing. The pews generally are in eighteenth century style. Somewhat earlier is a fine three-decker pulpit with cover. These pulpits date from the time when preaching was of supreme importance and the pulpit rather than the altar the focus of the church. They are now quite uncommon; long may Weston's remain.

Site: about two miles (3km) north-west of Otley on a minor road to Askwith. Turn left down a very narrow road where you see a grindstone, some stocks and a telephone box.
Grid Ref: SE 178466

A Village that Time Forgot

Buildings of the seventeenth and eighteenth centuries in the vernacular style can be seen everywhere in the Dales. They are the most valuable of all our Dales treasures.

The style has several characteristics. Windows have mullions and hoodmoulds above them to act as rain shields. Roofs have coping stones running down the slopes of the gables, the earlier ones often narrow. At the base of the coping stones

are heavy horizontal stones projecting from the walls ('kneelers') which act as a restraining stop for the copings and which are often decorated. On top of the kneelers one sometimes finds finials of varying shapes, eg spherical or pointed. Mullions, copings and kneelers may all be moulded, ie made with cross-sections which are not simply rectangular but partly convex or chamfered, particularly in the older houses. Doorheads are often dated and have elaborate carving.

The village of Clifton, off the beaten track and little known, has a collection of old houses of varying dates. Without exception they are well worth looking at.

Site: about two miles (3km) north of Otley on the road to Blubberhouses, turn left to Clifton.
Grid Ref: SE 193482

The Robinson Library

In 1851 Robinson Gill of Timble emigrated to New York. There he made his fortune and, in 1890, as president of no less than two banks he decided to help his native village and preserve an ancestral name.

On land provided by the Duchy of Lancaster, opposite the Timble Inn, he built the Robinson Library, gave £200 for books and an endowment of £2,000 for future maintenance.

The community centre flourished, but after Gill died in 1897 it was discovered that the invested £2,000 had not. The school closed in 1904, and although the library continued as a community centre for a while, the building deteriorated.

In such a tiny community that would normally have been the end, but the trustees resolved to raise funds for refurbishment and to keep the place going. They succeeded and the village still has its much-needed social centre.

Site: five miles (8km) north of Otley on a minor road to Blubberhouses, turn right at a Timble signpost.

Grid Ref: SE 179529

A House of Great Influence

Away from any motor road but easy of access by public footpath is a house which, from an architectural viewpoint, is one of the most important in the Dales.

Legend has it that a poor weaver called Robinson was in London during the great plague, made a fortune by robbing the bodies of the dead and their houses, brought his gold back to the Washburn and built Swinsty Hall.

The true story is rather more prosaic. It was indeed a man called Robinson who acquired the house, but it was in settlement of a debt owed by a certain Francis Wood, for whom the house was first built.

Be that as it may, Swinsty Hall was a landmark in Dales building, with features unusual for its time in these parts. It is an Elizabethan house from the 1570s, with mullioned and transomed windows of many lights, a single-story hall with a low gallery leading to a dining room, kitchens below and splendid roof-trusses. The porch is of three stories, its upper window having a raised centre light, a feature which became fashionable and was much copied thereafter in the Dales.

Site: the hall is about half a mile (0.8km) on a level track going south-east from the car park between Swinsty and Fewston reservoirs.

Grid Ref: SE 194532

Curious Gravestones

It is difficult to imagine Fewston Church as it was before the local reservoirs were built in the 1870s and a packed street of houses ran from it down the hillside to the River Washburn. Originally built in the fourteenth century, the nave and chancel were destroyed by fire in 1696, and the rebuilding of 1697 makes it one of very few churches from that time.

The visitor should not miss the treasures and

curiosities of the graveyard. There is a box tomb (left) dated 1613 which is very early for its type, and in the corner is an unusual low and broad headstone (below) thought to have been an imitation of the kind of wooden board once used as grave markers by poor people. Near the

porch is a gravestone with an inscription telling us that Joseph Ridstone died on the 29th February 1823 and his son died on the 30th February 1802, both of them dates which never existed. No one knows why.

Site: a short way east of Blubberhouses on the A59, a minor road leads to Fewston village.

Grid Ref: SE 195541

A Sunken Village

From the roadway which crosses Thruscross dam, the view is quite remarkable: 142 acres (57.5ha) of water surrounded by forest and farmland stretch away to the north-west up the valley of the River Washburn.

The maximum depth of the reservoir is about 120 feet (35m), and down in the depths lies the village of West End with its mills, farms, chapel and church, or at least what remains of them because the collapse of the local texile industry in the middle of the ninetenth century caused the village to be deserted and derelict long before the dam was built.

Many of the buildings had indeed been demolished and only a few houses continued to be occupied, though the church remained in use until shortly before the reservoir was finished, and was in fact the last building to be destroyed. At a trial filling of the reservoir in 1966 its bellcote remained visible and it was decided to reduce the church to its foundations. Now they appear only in times of drought. (The illustration shows the foundations of West End Church as revealed during recent droughts.) At other times, as you stand on the dam wall, you must imagine beneath the waves, a village which, church apart, was already dead when it was drowned.

Site: leaving Blubberhouses on the Greenhow Hill road, turn left in just over two miles (3km).

Grid Ref: SE 156575

Treasures Everywhere You Look

The Swo'dil

Sheep are just as much treasures in the Dales as any which are man-made. Vast flocks have lived here since mediaeval times, and have created its much-loved landscape by keeping the grass cropped and preventing the regrowth of trees. The Swaledale, easily identified by its greyish-white muzzle and black face, was officially

recognised as a separate breed in 1919. They are small and hardy with soft but very hard-wearing wool, and there are two million of them. It is quite appropriate that the Yorkshire Dales National Park chose a Swaledale tup (ram) as its emblem.

The hill farmers who maintain pure flocks have ewes which usually have only one lamb for, say, three or four years. They are often then sold to lower farms, where they are crossed with Teeswater tups to produce Masham lambs or with Blue-faced Leicesters to produce Mules. These cross-bred ewes may then go to better pastures still to produce fat lambs using Suffolk tups. Nearly all have twins.

The Dalesbred, the native sheep of North Craven distinguished by white flashes on each side of its nostrils, is bred from in a similar way.

Without the sheep we would no longer have the Dales as we know them.

A Maze of Walls

The beauty of the Dales landscape would be much diminished if it were not for the walls, such as these near the village of Kettlewell in Wharfedale. Sometimes in limestone, sometimes in gritstone and sometimes in both where the underlying rocks are in close proximity, they line roads and tracks, enclose irregular ancient fields near villages and farms, form boundaries to more regular but still rather small fields in the valleys, or march in straight lines over the high fells containing vast areas of rough grazing. The very long, straight walls date mainly from the late eighteenth and early nineteenth centuries, the height of the enclosure period. The irregular walls near settlements are the earliest, dating back to mediaeval times.

Their construction was more or less standardised. Each wall is essentially two walls leaning towards each other, the space between them being bridged by 'throughs' and otherwise packed with 'fillings'. The bases of each wall (the 'footings') are large, squarish boulders well bedded in the surface of the land with a total spread of about two and a half feet (75cm). The tops, with a spread of about one foot (30cm), are capped by a single stone. Many capping styles can be seen. Most commonly, the 'capstones' are thin semi-circular stones standing on their diameters, frequently all leaning in one dirction depending on the lie of the land. The total height is about five and a half feet (1.5m), and seven yards (6.5m) a day was expected of the waller, a somewhat daunting task requiring several tons of stone.

The easiest place to watch a modern waller and see his techniques is at one of the Dales shows, perhaps at Kilnsey in late August or Pateley Bridge in late September.

Lynchets

Visitors to the Dales are often intrigued by the field terraces and embankments which they see. They are lynchets, relics of ancient agriculture when growing grain and other crops was common. Most of them are believed to date from late mediaeval times — though some are undoubtedly older from the Anglian (pre-Norman) period — when ploughing by oxen with heavy ploughs on sloping ground was extremely difficult. Terraces, partly made by repeated ploughing in the same direction and partly deliberately made with embankments reinforced by stones, clearly made life easier. They also helped to preserve moisture and prevent erosion.

Some of the best examples are around Malham and in upper Wharfedale, but they exist almost everywhere apart from the far north-west, eg in upper Swaledale where the Norse settlers were pastoralists and did not grow crops. (Those pictured are to the north of Langcliffe in Ribblesdale.)

Lynchets are usually along contours, but not always, and when they go up and down steep slopes they present a puzzle that has not been satisfactorily explained.

Stepping Stones

Stepping stones are common in the Dales, many of them nowadays not easy to use except by the sure-footed and even then only when water levels are low. Most are on very old routes. Among the best known are those at Bolton Abbey, just above the footbridge, which must have been used by countless monks and others to pass between the abbey and Storiths. Upriver there are more near the foot of Hebden Beck below the suspension bridge, and there is yet another set near Linton Church.

Bad weather, bad light and the swiftly rising waters of the Wharfe no doubt made for many a hazardous crossing by the parishioners of Hebden on their way to church, and the erection of their own church in the early Victorian period must have been a great relief.

Near Dent is a place called Hippins, the old dialect word for stepping stones.

The stones illustrated are at Drebley (grid ref SE 058592).

Barns of the Dales

Without its barns the Dales would be a very different place. Many of them are old, dating from the seventeenth and eighteenth centuries, and they are also full of interest. Some were once houses; others had accommodation for farm hands. Some are vast buildings with threshing floors and housing for cows, horses and carts, while other small barns were built to house a handful of cattle and their feed.

These small barns — it sometimes seems as if there is one in every field — are a particular feature of Swaledale (as shown in the photo), where they operated as an almost closed economy. Cattle housed in a barn provided manure for the field in which it stood, and hay from the field was stored in the barn to provide food for those same cattle. The farmer with his backcan walked from the farm to milk the cows.

A typical small field barn might house four cows tethered in pairs to upright poles, called boskins, in stalls called booses. Behind them there was a walkway to facilitate cleaning and a mucking-out hole through which dung could be shovelled, and ahead of them was a passage (a foddergang) which enabled the farmer to provide feed. Beyond that was the hay store (the mew). When the barn was on sloping ground (such as this one in Langstrothdale), the mew might be above the cattle, with external access to it from higher up the slope and a trap door through which hay could be dropped.

Though no longer needed, at least for their original purpose, the National Park Authority is doing its best to preserve them. They are treasures in the landscape.

Limekilns

Some years ago the Dales historian Arthur Raistrick said that there were still 336 limekilns to be seen in Dentdale, Garsdale, and the upper reaches of Wharfedale and Wensleydale. In the whole of the Dales there are said to be over 1,000, and they can even be found on the lateral moraines of Ilkley Moor where glaciers deposited limestone on gritstone territory.

The kilns were built mainly in the eighteenth and nineteenth centuries, their function being to burn limestone to lime, which could be used either to make mortar for building or to spread on pastures which were excessively acid. (The kiln illustrated is on Threshfield Moor.)

Size and shape vary but basically they are all much the same, with a circular bowl tapering towards the base in which limestone and fuel would be stacked in alternate layers. There was a draw hole, usually facing south-west to get the best draught, and a grate from which burnt lime and ashes could be taken.

When you see a kiln, try and imagine what the Dales looked like when the lime-burning season was in full swing and hundreds of columns of smoke were rising from the fells. It must have been an amazing sight.

Bibliography

This collection of treasures might well have included some of the literature about the Dales written by those whose knowledge and love of the area shines through all that they wrote. Consciously or unconsciously it owes a great deal to them. It is not possible to list all their books individually, but I am thinking particularly of the work of Ella Pontefract and Marie Hartley, Marie Hartley and Joan Ingilby, Arthur Raistrick, Harry Speight and W R Mitchell. Different in kind but totally enjoyable and equally steeped in a love of the Dales are the works of Edmund Bogg. Perhaps not always entirely reliable in content, they are delightfully enriched by the illustrations of the artists associated with him.

For a rather earlier view of the Dales, I recommend:

Chronicles and Stories of the Craven Dales by J H Dixon (1881).

Rambles in Upper Wharfedale by B J Harker (1869).

A Month in Yorkshire by Walter White (1858).

and even earlier, but towering over all else for the scope of its historical research, is:

The History and Antiquities of the Deanery of Craven by Dr T D Whitaker (1805).

For architectural information, the Buildings of England series of Nikolaus Pevsner for the West Riding and North Riding are unequalled for their comprehensiveness and scholarship.

A number of novelists have written about the Dales, including William Riley (*Men of Mawm*, *Jerry and Ben* etc), C J Cutcliffe Hyne and, much earlier, Mary Howitt, but in my view the outstanding Dales novel is Thomas Armstrong's *Adam Brunskill* which vividly recreates the life of the Swaledale leadminer.

The work of local dialect poets may not be easy to read (or indeed at all easy to obtain), but if you can get hold of them by hook or by crook the works of Tom Twistleton, John Thwaite and Thomas Blackah will illuminate your understanding of the Dales and the Dalesman better than many more famous works.

Finally I must mention a few other books which I have consulted:

Roman Ilkley by B R Hartley.

Ilkley: The Victorian Era by David Carpenter.

Eminent Victorians (about W E Forster) by M & D Warwick.

The song of Upper Wharfedale edited by T Sharpe (a City of Bradford publication).

Village Schools by Elizabeth Raistrick.

Kit Calvert of Wensleydale by T C Calvert.

Regretfully I have to say that not all of these books are easily obtainable.

Index